MALCOLM LOWRY
HIS ART AND EARLY LIFE
A study in transformation

MALCOLM LOWRY
HIS ART & EARLY LIFE

A study in transformation

M. C. BRADBROOK

Mistress of Girton College and Professor of
English in the University of Cambridge

813
54
LOWRY

CAMBRIDGE UNIVERSITY PRESS

Published by the Syndics of the Cambridge University Press
Bentley House, 200 Euston Road, London NW1 2DB
American Branch: 32 East 57th Street, New York, N.Y. 10022

Library of Congress Catalogue Card Number: 74–76945

ISBN: 0 521 20473 9

First Published 1974

Printed in Great Britain by
Western Printing Services Ltd, Bristol

CONTENTS

MAPS

ACKNOWLEDGEMENTS

My thanks are due to Mrs Margerie Bonner Lowry and the Executors of the Malcolm Lowry Estate for permission to quote from the works of Malcolm Lowry, and in particular to reprint the two short stories from *The Fortnightly*, the Leys School magazine. Acknowledgement is also due to the following for permission to quote copyright material: Jonathan Cape Ltd and A. D. Peters and Company for extracts from *Under the Volcano, Dark as the Grave wherein my Friend is Laid* (edited by Douglas Day and Margerie Bonner Lowry), *Lunar Caustic, Hear us, O Lord, from Heaven thy Dwelling Place, October Ferry to Gabriola* (edited by Margerie Bonner Lowry), and *Ultramarine*; to A. D. Peters and Company and City Lights Books, San Francisco, for extracts from *Selected Poems*; and to A. D. Peters and Company for extracts from *The Selected Letters of Malcolm Lowry*, edited by Harvey Breit and Margerie Bonner Lowry. The Librarian of the Special Collections at the University of British Columbia and the Liverpool City Librarian have given leave to quote from material in their keeping. The Headmaster of the Leys School has kindly agreed to the publication of the two short stories.

I am obliged to Douglas Day for his assistance in obtaining in advance a copy of *Malcolm Lowry, a Biography* (New York, Oxford University Press, 1973).

Mr and Mrs Wilfrid Lowry and Mr Russell Lowry have greatly helped me by their recollections; Russell Lowry read the proofs. Others to whom I am endebted are I. A. Richards, Julian Trevelyan, Kathleen Raine, the Fellows and Former Manciple of St Catharine's College, and Guy Wilcockson of Pembroke College, formerly of the Leys School staff. For Canadian material I am obliged to Graham Spry of Ottawa and William H. New of the University of British Columbia. Among members of my college who have helped, Sheila Gillies spent some time checking MSS at the University of British Columbia, Ann Parr drew the maps, and Pat Rignold gave unwearying readiness in typing, checking

Acknowledgements

and hunting references, as well as contributing from her knowledge of Merseyside.

The page references to novels and tales in the text are to the latest editions by Jonathan Cape, except for *Under the Volcano*, where I have used the page references of the Penguin Modern Classics edition, for the convenience of the general reader.

Cambridge   M. C. Bradbrook
February 1974

EXILE, DEATH AND LIFE

(from the Norwegian of Nordahl Grieg)

Dark looms the rock in the sea,
Barren, cold and lone.
It is Norway now,
All we may call our own.

Storms rage in perpetual night,
Mists swirl in the summer gale,
Thrashing desolate earth—
Icicle, rock and shale.

This is our world, our home . . .
But slowly we took our mould,
Our minds formed in likeness of
The land we no longer hold.

Blossom, woodland and grass
Dowered sap and calm of their own;
So we must bleed with all
Life that is trampled down.

. . .

So that a second race,
Flowering warm and free,
Leafy-and-corn embowered,
Is spared being such as we.
                    Øya i Ishavet (The Polar Rock)

The best haven't got any future,
The best have only to die.
                    De Beste (The Best)

You were the bird wings
Over white islands,
The heather that flames
By the beck far away,
The bird-song in springtime,
The wood's winter stillness
– You, in my heart
A pure, clear spring.
            Gerd (Dedicatory poem for *Friheten*,
                Reykjavik, 1943)

CHRONOLOGY

The early life of Malcolm Lowry

Arthur Osborne Lowry, cotton-broker (1870–1945) married Evelyn Boden (1873–1950), daughter of Captain Boden of Liverpool (d. 1880); 4 sons: Stuart Osborne Lowry (1895–1969); Wilfrid Malbon Lowry, b. 1900; Arthur Russell Lowry, b. 1905; Clarence Malcolm Lowry, b. 28 July 1909 at Warren Crest, North Drive, New Brighton, Cheshire, d. at The White Cottage, Ripe, Sussex, 27 June 1957.

1911 Family moved to newly built home, Inglewood, Caldy, Wirral, Cheshire.

1914– Stuart Lowry served with the Royal Welch Fusiliers, 18   crippled in foot.

1915 Malcolm at a local school.

1917 Malcolm goes to prep. school for the Leys (Caldicott, Hitchin).

1918 Malcolm taken to see a 'Q' ship in Liverpool docks by his brother Wilfrid.

1919 Stuart Lowry marries, goes to Texas.

1920 Wilfrid capped for England at Rugby.

1923 Malcolm goes to the Leys School (West House), Cambridge.

1924 Stuart Lowry returns; Malcolm wins a golf championship for boys at the Royal Liverpool Golf Links, Hoylake.

1925 Wilfrid marries and leaves home. Stuart introduces Malcolm to the works of Balzac, Joyce, O'Neill, etc. Malcolm publishes first story in *The Fortnightly* (March), writes *A Rainy Night* (October).

1926 Malcolm begins to write scathing hockey reports; writes *Satan in a Barrel*. Goes on tour of France with hockey team (Easter). Wins prize for verse.

1927 Malcolm leaves school in Form V Remove (Easter), sails on 17 May from Liverpool as deck-hand in *s.s. Pyrrhus*, a 'Blue Piper' freighter of the Blue Funnel Line, for Yokohama via Port Said and Penang; returns in October.

1928 Goes to English College at Bonn (January–March). Meets Paul Fitte?

Chronology

1929   Goes to New England to spend summer with Conrad
        Aiken. October: goes up to St Catharine's College Cam-
        bridge. 14 November: suicide of Paul Fitte. Malcolm
        witness at inquest.

1930?   At his birthday party, responding to his father's toast,
        Malcolm says his childhood had been one of gloom, blind-
        ness, etc. July–Sept. goes to Norway on a freighter.

1930–   Publications at Cambridge include *Goya the Obscure* (*The
31   Venture*, no. 6), *Port Swettenham* (*Experiment*, no. 4),
        and *Punctum indifferens; skibet gaar videre* (*Experiment*,
        no. 7). English Tripos Part I, Class III.

1932   June: English Tripos Part II, Class III. Severe break with
        family. Goes to London, then to Paris.

1933   Publication of *Ultramarine* by Jonathan Cape. Leaves for
        Spain with Conrad Aiken, who draws Lowry's allowance
        for him (April–June). Meets Jan Gabrial, a 'stunt girl'
        from Hollywood films, in Granada.

1934   Marries Jan Gabrial in Paris (14th arrondissement) 6
        January, witness: Julian Trevelyan, who draws Lowry's
        allowance for him. Jan leaves for New York after about
        6 months. Malcolm returns to London. October: Goes alone
        to New York.

Summary of later years

1935   June: spends ten days in psychiatric wing of Bellevue
        Hospital, New York. Begins *Lunar Caustic*, first draft.

1936   December: arrives in Cuernavaca with Jan via Los Angeles.
        Begins *Under the Volcano*.

1937   September: Aiken visits Cuernavaca. December: Jan leaves
        Lowry finally. Oaxaca, friendship with Juan Fernando
        Márquez. In jail.

1938   Acapulco, Mexico City. July: goes to Los Angeles. Begins
        second draft of *Under the Volcano*.

1939   7 June: meets Margerie Bonner. July: leaves for Vancouver.
        Joined by Margerie. Begins third draft of *Under the
        Volcano*.

1940   August: moves to Dollarton. Divorce made absolute. Marries
        Margerie Bonner 2 December.

1944   7 June: Dollarton home burnt. Leaves for Niagara-on-the-
        Lake. Completion of *Under the Volcano*, Christmas Eve.

1945   February: returns to rebuild home. February: death of
        Arthur Lowry. 28 November: returns to Mexico to write
        Dark as the Grave.

1946   8 March: arrested for debt of former fine from 1938.
        6 April: *Under the Volcano* accepted. 4 May: deported,

returns to Vancouver. November: leaves for New Orleans. 26 December: sails for Haiti.

1947   February: to New York via Miami. 19 February: *Under the Volcano* published. Returns to Vancouver. 7 November: sails to Europe via Panama; arrives 23 December.

1948   In Paris; Cassis; in hospital in Paris. Travels to Italy and Brittany.

1949   Flies to Canada. Works on stories and novels. July: in hospital after fall from pier.

1950   December: death of Evelyn Lowry.

1954   January: connection with American publisher severed. August: leaves Dollarton finally; reaches Sicily in November, via New York.

1955   June: arrives in London. November: in hospital, for psychiatric treatment.

1956   February: settles at Ripe. Starts work again.

1957   June: in Lake District. 27 June: death in Ripe.

Perfection of the life or of the work?

The intellect of man is forced to choose
Perfection of the life or of the work:
And if it choose the second, must refuse
A heavenly mansion, raging in the dark.

W. B. Yeats

Malcolm Lowry is at this time recognised as one of the greatest novelists of the twentieth century; without doubt the greatest novelist (except possibly E. M. Forster) whom Cambridge has produced. The relation of his works to his biography poses problems of more than personal significance. The importance of his early life in shaping his work cannot be gauged without considering both the conventions of his art and the facts, in so far as they can be established. As a contemporary of Lowry at Cambridge, raised in the same intellectual climate – and as someone who was born in the same town and the same year, with a very similar if less affluent background – I have tried to rebuild the shaping impulses of those earlier years, whilst recognising that the creative energies that transformed them belonged to another time and another place.

The general shape of Lowry's life is known from his novels; he has depicted as central figures a young seaman (*Ultramarine*), an alcoholic (the Consul, hero of *Under the Volcano*, his greatest work), and a writer who lived in a beach shack on Vancouver Bay (Sigbjørn Wilderness). Any crude and reductive approach to these figures does less than justice to the art which created them. Lowry was also a poet, and in many ways he anticipated the interests of our own time. His concern for conservation of the environment, his crusade against pollution, belong to the seventies. Like Blake's, his landscape

1

N

Bootle

New Brighton

Wallasey

Liverpool

Leasowe

Hoylake

Moreton

Hilbre

Birkenhead

Caldy

R. Mersey

R. Dee

600

Clwydian
Range

Scale 1:126,720
Ferry and bus routes - - - - -

1. LIVERPOOL BAY

depicts 'two contrary states of the human soul' – beatitude and despair, heaven and hell. He lived the life of a 'hippie' and drop-out before the colonies of Big Sur and Venice West were established further down the Pacific coast. His favourite author, Hermann Hesse, is being newly discovered by the youth of the seventies. His own works too are being increasingly accepted. The present study attempts to bring out their underlying unity, and especially the power of the latest work, reflecting as it does the integration of life and reading; its apparent disintegration is the price of deepening art.

The kindness of Douglas Day supplied an advance copy of *Malcolm Lowry, a Biography*,[1] a study whose heroic proportions result from seven years' work, besides incorporating the work of a predecessor, Conrad Knickerbocker who died in 1966.

Day presents his work as the life of the author of *Under the Volcano*, for he pauses in his narrative to discuss at length the second draft and the published version. His narrative opens, like the novel, with the death of its hero, and reverts to the beginnings of Lowry's life only on p. 52. The shaping idea behind the novel Day sees as that of Cocteau's play on Oedipus, *La Machine Infernale*; this same power seems to impel the grim acceleration of Lowry's alcoholic progress to its inevitable end.

> Behold, spectator, wound up to the full, so that its spring slowly uncoils throughout the length of human life, one of the most perfect machines built by the gods of the abyss for the mathematical destruction of a human life.[2]

Malcolm Lowry began drinking at school and, with two short intermissions, went on drinking for the rest of his life. The first intermission, following his marriage to

Margerie Bonner, lasted for about four years, from 1940 till the burning of his Vancouver waterside home in June 1944, when he had virtually finished the last draft of *Under the Volcano*. The second intermission, from February 1956 to his death, was spent in Sussex, where he worked on *October Ferry to Gabriola*, and the short stories in *Hear Us O Lord from Heaven thy Dwelling Place*. In May 1957 his wife told his doctor that his condition was fine; and a month later a last disastrous drinking bout ended in suicide (or more charitably 'Death by misadventure').

The end becomes predictable as the story unfolds; moments of violence – Lowry made several earlier attempts at suicide and two or three murderous attacks on his wife – are balanced by the stoic endurance with which he accepted an appalling early variety of aversion treatment, and was even willing to face more of it. Lowry's powers of physical recovery astonished and sometimes deceived his doctors; at the worst time he could write witty letters, and his sense of humour remained. A handful of friends, and his wife, kept him from despair; when in the last year of his life she collapsed under stress, he wrote sensitively and sensibly to her family, and looked after her during her convalescence.

However, Day has little material for a literary life in the ordinary sense of the word, since Lowry was at first from shyness unwilling, and finally incapable of living in the world. Even his spiritual father Conrad Aiken faded out of his life quite early; he drew on the writers of the past, for the community of the dead gave him an alternative world (including his dead friends); some people had not realised they played any great part in his life.[3] When he took his first voyage as a seventeen-year-old schoolboy, his mother told a newspaper reporter 'He is bent on a literary career, and his short story writing is all to him';

in later years his doctor Sir Paul Mallinson confirmed this 'His life was so lopsided. If his writing was not going well, his life was not worth living.' (Day, p. 91, p. 30.)

When he was being urged to seek the help of a psycho-analyst, his friend, the painter Julian Trevelyan told him that he did not need psychoanalysis, he needed to write.

The judgement that all his books are disguised auto-biography ignores the shaping power that appeared con-structive and free in his books while his life became ruinous and self-destructive. At the end, when fantasies played an increasing part in ordinary life, the truth emerged symbolically in fiction, especially in uncovered symbols of his earliest years.

Never was there a better illustration of Eliot's dictum 'The more perfect the artist, the more completely separate in him will be the man who suffers and the mind which creates.' It is precisely because of the autobiographical element in his work that the artist in Lowry must be remembered; if in life he indulged in fantasies, in his art he could be ruthless in his own self-depiction:

It was melancholy to hear him try to shift
The blame on us for his sure guilt; but gift
Of clarity he lacked . . .
When the doomed are most eloquent in their sinking
It seems that then we are least strong to save . . .

The metaphor confers a godlike detachment[4] while the statement depicts a hopeless case. Lowry could read the compass but he could not change his course.

However, he could attain not only the visionary power of seeing a world bent on destruction, imaged in the death of one man, the Consul, but could weigh up political issues shrewdly. A very late essay, according to Day,

5

contains 'a surprisingly astute treatise on the evils of McCarthyism and the responsibilities of freedom'. He had a phenomenal memory, testified to by his brothers and friends from all periods of his life. James Stern described how on their meeting after a fourteen years' gap, Lowry recalled a remark which he might have been thought incapable of hearing, since he had apparently fallen insensible to the floor – 'Why did you tell that pretty girl, who was probably your sister, that I was DRUNK?' was his greeting to his old friend.

He himself was haunted and sometimes frightened by his own powers of recall and association, connecting them with some kind of magic 'correspondences' in the world. The phenomenon which Jung described as 'synchronicity', and which was much studied by one of Lowry's favourite authors, Charles Fort, is always unpredictable; such psychic 'explosions' stand in full opposition to the only-too-predictable course of Lowry's alcoholic deterioration.

It is the last which Douglas Day has concentrated on, as any biographer was bound to do. His psychological interpretation (pp. 61–74) is not reductive, and in an epilogue he declares that Lowry's genius, which lay not in his failure as a man but in his achievement as an artist, cannot be explained or circumscribed by his neuroses. On the other hand, he does believe that the neuroses eventually inhibited and disrupted his art. Freud on the presence of a harsh threatening superego, accounting for 'self punitive drinking and impairment of potency both genital and creative' may seem to fit the case; especially if it is linked, as Day links it, with striking elements of infantilism – an inability to distinguish between the self and the world, which is characteristic of disturbance at the earliest, oral stage of infancy. Lowry himself was expert at such diagnosis, as he shows ironically in *Lunar Caustic* ('return to the presexual revives the necessity for nutrition'). The second draft of *Under the Volcano* applies the expected terms to the hero (which in the final version are removed):

> It was as though the passionate narcissism which drink-ing and his almost purely oral response to life entailed had fixed his age at some time in the past, at the unidentifiable moment, perhaps, when his persistent objective self, weary of standing askance and watching his downfall, had silently withdrawn from him alto-gether, like a ship secretly leaving harbour at night.[5]

Any critic who attempts to apply psychiatric categories to an author is handicapped by the fact that his own make-up will be part of his reaction, and what he sees will be selected from the field partly in accordance with his own reactions. Only if there is a wide critical consensus can this be avoided. Secondly, it is very much easier to apply such categories to unsuccessful than to successful works.

Lowry was in this way peculiarly defenceless; in his undergraduate days a student magazine depicted him curled up inside the body of a ukelele as if in a womb. Probably the worst of Lowry's published works – it appeared without his knowledge – is a short story en-titled 'Economic Conference, 1934'.[6] It is a gift to the reductive expositor.

In a Bacchanalian scene between a taximan and an American journalist it is resolved to dismiss the whole political and economic dilemma of Europe, while in a drunken song Lowry in effect proclaims in childish terms his intentions of indulging in the largest oral consumption of which he is capable at his father's expense.

> Father of mine awaken I pray thee to the truth
> Two helps of eggs and bacon are requisite for youth

7

And since thy little nipper needs much more food than
thee Deny thyself that kipper and hand it on to me
(That's swell said Bill) The meal no longer swell is
Dad chuck across that toast For at last my empty
stomach says that I should rule the roast Hunger
must have its qualms allayed Beyond my wildest
dream Go easy with the marmalade Let me
scrape out the cream Pile up my platter rather
Than thine with chunks of pine Because my need dear
father Is greater far than thine.

A punitive superego indeed! In the margin of an unpublished tale about the return from a voyage is written
'What I remember chiefly is that the wharf got nearer
and nearer while my father loomed larger and larger.'[7]

'Economic Conference, 1934', that gift to the amateur
psychiatrist, not only features the two drunks, both named
Bill, and both having three brothers – but one set is
dead – it is placed in a cabby's kip full of glass cases of
little dead stuffed animals,[8] and even a stuffed dead
Chinaman. But beyond this level it has (as writing) no
interest at all.

After his drifting from his own family in 1932 when
he was twenty-three, Lowry seems to have sought family
ties with other groups of brothers – to have talked about
his own family, particularly about his father, to the point
of boredom.[9] In his stories his parents and brothers
appeared in 'displaced' and often hostile forms.[10] Under
drug treatment, later in life, he revealed even stronger
displacement fantasies.[11] All this, however, belongs to
the life, and not to the work. There were other qualities
in Lowry's daily life, of a more attractive kind.

Douglas Day states very pithily the difficulties of a
biographer:

8

Perfection of the life or of the work?

Why were so many dissimilar people so utterly con-
vinced of the brilliance of Malcolm Lowry, before there
was any evidence of that brilliance? Apparently, when
Lowry was in a good mood . . . he could be so full of
joyous energy that the word 'genius' seemed the only
appropriate word for him. Unhappily for the biographer, there is no way of recording this quality or of
transmitting it; one simply accepts it as a matter of
faith. (p. 127)

To the end brilliance can be found – in the letters most
readily but in the other works fitfully. Only one or two
stories capture the absurd high spirits of early days, and
sometimes even then, the overtones are macabre, as in the
anecdote of how Lowry walked into the deep end of the
swimming pool at Haiti (Day, p. 374).

Ara Calder-Marshall, wife of a friend from the early
thirties, testifies:

Whatever state Malc was in, he was splendidly good
natured about it. Somehow, I always thought of a fox.
Right, they've run me to earth. Then, in a flash, he'd be
away, through the gents, miraculously disappearing
again, anywhere – anywhere to go on with his mar-
vellous mind.[12]

In north country dialect, a Lowry *is* a red fox, which,
being as sensitive as he was to the quality of names, particularly his own, Malcolm Lowry could not have failed
to appreciate.[13] Mischievous, adept at disguises and at
playing a part, predatory, excessively energetic, the red-
haired quarry still to some extent eludes the pursuit of
the most dedicated biographer. A careful and judicious
reconstruction, supported by a wealth of quotation, testi-
mony, photographs, and very finely balanced judgement,

Day's *Life*, with the exception of some of the early parts, is a job done once for all. But the picture that emerges is the determinist one of the drunkard's inexorable progress, the operation of the Infernal Machine. This, perhaps is inevitable, if the task is approached through the later years, where the documentation is fullest.

Day is concerned not only with the biographical facts but also with the interrelation of *Under the Volcano*; he follows his biographical review of what happened to Lowry during his stay in Mexico 1936–8 with an account of the second draft of this book (the first draft has disappeared) and on the occasion of the second visit to Mexico Day returns to an account of the final version,[14] with an analysis upon five different levels.

The first draft was written while Lowry was actually in Mexico; the second draft was begun in Hollywood in 1939, and completed in Vancouver in the following year. Early in 1937 the germ of the novel had emerged in a short story, also called *Under the Volcano*, based on an incident which derived from experience, according to Lowry. It tells the story of the bus ride in which passengers encounter but fail to succour a robbed and dying traveller, the substance of what was to be chapter VIII of the novel. The Consul, Hugh and Yvonne, the three chief characters appear, but Yvonne is the Consul's daughter, not his wife, and the younger man is her fiancé.

The second draft still, like the original short story, shows the heroine as the Consul's daughter, not his wife, who had been educated, chiefly in the facts of life, at Girton College Cambridge; it stresses much more heavily political references to the war in Spain, and is without the mythic density of image by which, Day observes, *Under the Volcano* became 'not a novel at all, but a kind

10

of monument to prodigality of vision' (p. 270). Yet the Consul is already a figure of superhuman significance

> Suppose that all the suffering and chaos and conflict of the present were suddenly to take human form . . . a man to whom, like Jesus, the great betrayal of the human spirit would appear in the guise of a private, anguishing betrayal . . . all these horrors of today had suddenly convulsed upon themselves to create a soul, and that soul had sought a body, and the only body it had found sufficiently photophobic for its purpose was the Consul's. (Day, p. 259 from p. 4 of draft)

Day thinks that it is a mistake to try to isolate the strands instead of taking the *Gestalt* of this work; it is a mistake to look too hard for traces of 'Aiken and Joyce and Dante and Aztec mythology and Shelley and Elizabethan poetry and Swedenborg and the expressionist films of Robert Wiene . . .'. The five levels that Day discerns in the book, all pointing towards the inevitable conclusion, are the chthonic or earthbound level; the landscape itself, demonic and sinister, including the last *cantina*, the Farolito, which is like an entry to a labyrinth. Signs and posters send out ominous messages. The second, the human level, centres round four chief characters, Geoffrey and Hugh Firmin, Yvonne, Geoffrey's wife, and Jacques Laruelle. The third level, the political, is 'still mimetically oriented'; this culminates in chapter x in the argument between the two brothers; the fourth level is the magical, the level at which the interweavings of the cabbala and the idea of Geoffrey as some sort of 'black magician' operate – he is Faustian as well as being Promethean; the last is the religious level.

Others, such as Dale Edmonds and Tony Kilgallin, have analysed the various levels of the work.[15]

Kilgallin's close reading of *Under the Volcano* depends on tracking some hundreds of literary echoes, of precisely the kind that Day rejects, whose ironic or absurdist resonances give depth and power to the prose; puns, thematic links; above all the cabbalist interpretation of nature can be detected only by the patient discovery of the original context, from which Lowry pillaged, in the manner of Eliot and Joyce. Charles Stansfeld-Jones, the cabbalist, for example, wrote on Parzival, the Wise Fool, who becomes a figure of great power in this and later writings. The opening chapter establishes the significance of the film producer Laruelle, who, like Conrad's Marlow, presides over the whole tale as a shaping figure – here the relevance of Eisenstein's *Thunder over Mexico*, with its epilogue of the *Day of the Dead*, and of other films extends the frontiers beyond literature into another art. *Ultramarine*, the only other book considered by Kilgallin, had established the Conradian balance between random yarns of the seamen, and the artist's symbolic technique. His brief biographic impressions fill out details from Vancouver and Dollarton acquaintances, certain episodes appearing in flat contradiction to the versions given by Day.

By showing what a mass of associations spread out from the close texture of *Under the Volcano*, Kilgallin implies that in spite of the book's firm structure, individual response will be open and various.

A blend of spontaneity and control produced in the end something that in one sense is like oral literature; it can work at all sorts of levels, and in different combinations of emphasis for different people. The later works retain even less of the novel form; Day terms them meditations. Yet on balance he regards these new forms as deterioration, their graces only the graces of fatigue (p. 470). While allowing full stature to *Lunar Caustic* and 'The

Forest Path to the Spring', he is ready to dismiss most of the rest of the work. In recording Lowry's view that his last writings were going to be as good as *Under the Volcano* the biographer adds: 'Were they? the answer is simple; no, not even close' (p. 437).

This challenge demands an equal directness; the answer is perhaps not quite so simple. Lowry's first novel established itself slowly, and, as Wordsworth knew, every true artist creates the taste by which he is appreciated. The later works belong to the present day or perhaps the future.

In the latest works, I would see a partial emergence, amid much that is shapeless, mistaken or sadly repetitive, of a new form. Two unfinished tales, 'Ghostkeeper' and 'The Ordeal of Sigbjørn Wilderness' are very plainly dictations to Margerie Lowry, for towards the end of his time in Canada, round 1953, Lowry experienced a psychological block which prevented him from holding a pen. This adds to their 'oral' effect; they become like ballads or seamen's yarns. Both are filled with evocations of the past; in the first the shores of Vancouver Bay remind the hero of his birthplace, New Brighton, England (Lowry's birthplace too) whilst the second opens with a letter to Lowry's supervisor at St Catharine's College Cambridge. Both these tales carry a strong flavour of the supernatural and the first was intended for inclusion in *Hear Us O Lord*, where it would form a kind of infernal parallel to 'The Bravest Boat'.[16] Another story, directly recalling his home on the Wirral peninsula and his public school is 'Enter One in Sumptuous Armour'. Clearly Lowry was working through his stories towards reintegrating his 'past' with his 'present'. Such indeed is the constant theme of these last works. All the different heroes, who are different aspects of Lowry, join to make the complete, nameless man, the hero of the last and greatest story, and perhaps the finest thing Lowry wrote, 'The Forest Path to the Spring'. But this character has been created by the book itself, has emerged out of the 'aeolian' unit of the tales, the unconscious blending of different aspects into a unity. The structure is only to be felt, sensed in the reading, or rather the internal reciting, of the stories. The 'unheard melody' as Keats would term it, depends on the apparently 'loose' germinative form.

The question is, if this method of integrating the self works for Lowry, does it work for anyone else? For the sympathetic reader, it does.[17]

Lowry practised an exact and literal fidelity in describing the natural world; some things had to be accurate. Yet he excelled in giving mist and colour, light slanted across water or leaves; the objects are symbolic rather than emblematic; they could not be lifted up and used elsewhere but belong to their context.

That context includes the real past. Here, without attempting to compete with the labours of Douglas Day, I may claim that fortune has given me the advantage of being able to correct and supplement the earlier parts of the biography. This, chiefly in order to present an alternative view of the late works, since my aim is not biographical but critical. To have lived in both the vanished worlds of Lowry's youth – that of the Liverpool seamen and the Wirral countryside, followed by the Cambridge of the late twenties and early thirties – may simply mean that I am projecting my own memories into Lowry's work. Yet these scenes exerted a powerful influence on him, which since the scenes change with the years is becoming difficult to recapture: to set down impressions may offer opportunities for re-interpretation to others.

To take one simple point, Lowry habitually refers to his

14

father as 'the Old Man', which Day equates with God (p. 349); but it is the regular term of a ship's crew for the Master. The Wirral scene that Lowry knew was not as Day pictures it; New Brighton had lost its tawdriness and had not yet been battered, whilst Birkenhead, far from being a 'failed boom town', was one of the two or three greatest shipbuilding centres in England.

The Cambridge of Lowry's youth was such an exciting place that in spite of his admitted neglect of academic studies I have added an epilogue to try to present the scene in which he made lifelong friends – Gerald Noxon, John Davenport, Martin Case – where he met Michael Redgrave and the Haldanes. Besides the official review list, only two copies of *Under the Volcano* were despatched on publication – one was to Conrad Aiken, the other to Michael Redgrave 'the actor, an old and good college friend of mine', publisher of one of his earliest stories.

Biography, then, is a useful tool, as it supplies a measure of the transformation that history underwent in Lowry's art. The suicide of Paul Fitte in his first term at college, the story of Lowry's relations with Charlotte Haldane, and the society that encouraged him to finish his first novel were part of the makings of the writer whose full significance is perhaps even yet not disclosed.

Lowry offered a natural subject for other writers. In 1932, he appeared at the centre of Charlotte Haldane's novel, *I Bring Not Peace*, in spite of the conventional disclaimer that no reference to any living person was intended. The book is dedicated to him and quotes some of his lyrics. His friend John Sommerfield depicted him in *The Last Weekend* as David Nordall (Day, p. 153; Kilgallin, p. 28, states that the MS of this unpublished novel was lent to a former official biographer, who failed to return it). His first wife, Jan Gabrial, depicted their parting

15

in a short story named 'Not with a Bang' (Day, pp. 230–233).

Now his works, not the man, are beginning to exercise a direct shaping influence; in his latest novel, Graham Greene, that very sensitive reflector, has adapted for his own purposes some of the features of *Under the Volcano*, as thematic basis for *The Honorary Consul* (1973).

1

Lowry's Eridanus

A shilling life will give you all the facts (W. H. Auden)

The author of *Under the Volcano* built from transformed memories, shaped by the craft of earlier masters in words; the blend of experience and craft is at its densest here. While technically unfinished, the best of his late works capture – in their 'gaps' – the disruptive struggle, the receding of continuously deepening vision which is their theme.

If Lowry's two 'Tyrannies', as he termed them, the pen and the bottle, possessed him utterly at times, he succeeded in building a life of allegory; in spite of the obvious relevance of his history to his artefacts (shown by Day), Lowry thus becomes the best possible interpreter of Lowry. Since events can be significant only in the context of his art, the purpose of these pages is to establish the conventions of the art itself. For his later life, Lowry's letters form his own chronicle;[1] his early life, which was progressively recovered and blended into the deepening vision of his latest works, can be traced from its transient historic form only through partial records and memories; but these suffice to show its continuous presence, though in a subjective form, i.e. Lowry's recovered past is always a symbolic past.

Only by following through the whole development, can Lowry be read as he asked; it is for this reason that the final chapters of the present work return to the historic facts of his youth, in the context supplied by the writing,

17

the facts being for posterity primarily sources for the work.

Lowry's conflicts and achievements can be traced to the time when at the age of sixteen he became absorbed in weaving a blend of recollection and fantasy, and dropped out of the competitive world of sport and social conformity. By this time too, at least one of his contemporaries had observed that drink had taken a firm hold of him.[2] His first novel, *Ultramarine*, established the theme of conflict between home and exile, in terms of a quest. *Under the Volcano* transforms one of the two 'Tyrannies', the tales of Sigbjørn Wilderness the other. At the deepest level, *October Ferry* returns to the linked themes of exile and suicide; the development of Lowry's work therefore shows the unity he claimed for it, when he named the whole sequence *The Voyage that never Ends*[3] – a unity of the 'aeolian' kind, exemplified in minuscule in his collection of short stories, *Hear Us O Lord*.

The youngest of a family of four brothers, born into the solid world of prosperous trading Liverpool, Lowry reached his eighteenth birthday in the course of a romantic voyage to Yokohama as bosun's boy on a freighter (May–October 1927). His success as a jazz musician won him a third reputation, which with those of a writer and drinker were all consolidated at Cambridge University (1929–32). Although resenting the pressure of conformity there, he completed his first novel, sat the English Tripos, and on the strength of the tales he submitted[4] achieved an honours degree. Otherwise, though 'obviously brilliant' in the eyes of one examiner at least, he would have failed. Immediately, in the summer of 1932, he began his long exile. The pattern of success broke up in wandering through Spain, Paris, New York, Mexico – as one of his fragments of verse confessed:

Some years ago he started to escape
. . . has been . . . escaping ever since . . .
          Some tell
Strange hellish tales of this poor founder'd soul
Who once fled north . . .
                    (*Under the Volcano*, p. 331)

Heavier and heavier drinking, a broken marriage, ten days in a mental hospital in New York, the political darkness of the Spanish Civil War, a Mexican jail, were succeeded by a chance settlement in British Columbia, a happy second marriage. Turning his back on the city and the world, accepting the wilderness (yet without aliena- tion or the embittered violence of later prophets of counter-culture), in his beach shack at Dollarton, Lowry reworked the life material from his Ishmael years 1932– 1940, in the fourteen years of what he recognised as his best writing (1940–54). His last three years in exile in Sicily and England were consumed in struggles with his daimon to embody the force that clamoured and tore at him – 'I am managing to eat it a little more than it eats me so far.' This was a posthumous existence; the life that devoured his energies now lay in the past. He died on 27 June 1957, a month short of his forty-eighth birthday, after a fatal mixture of gin and sodium amytol: the coroner's verdict was 'Death by misadventure'.

His first biographer, Conrad Knickerbocker, declared that Lowry could not perform the vital surgery of separa- ting himself from his characters 'save in the one book where he achieved a triumph of consciousness, expressed with the utmost lucidity'. His second biographer agrees (Day, p. 469). *Under the Volcano*, which by 1946 had taken shape, was explained structurally by Lowry in the lengthy letter he wrote to his publisher, Jonathan Cape;[5] later, he defended his work explicitly against being

considered autobiographical (*Letters*, pp. 329–44), con-
demned the realistic novel, and – apropos a friend's plan
for a structure based on different levels of consciousness –
declared: 'It never occurred to me that consciousness
itself could be of any aid, quite the contrary, let alone a
goal, Man forget yourself having been too often my
motto . . . All aboard for the good ship Solipsism and don't
forget your seaboots.'[6] 'Throw away your mind', the advice
given in his novels by good doctors,[7] implies that Lowry's
genius was in deep ways receptive, feminine and intuitive;
the more frequent charge, and one he feared, was not
autobiography but plagiarism. He was drawn to the sea
as much by reading Eugene O'Neill's *The Hairy Ape* and
Moon of the Caribbees, as by the family ties of his
maternal grandfather, the Liverpool sea captain. The discovery of Conrad Aiken's *Blue Voyage* prompted him
to write to the author, and in the summer of 1929 to cross
the Atlantic to learn from him the craft of writing. Conrad
Aiken's own fictional account, given years later in *Ushant*,
is itself a powerful tribute to the young author's conquer-
ing charm:

> that most engaging and volatile and unpredictable of
> geniuses; for surely of all the literary folk . . . there had
> been none among them, who had been so visibly or
> happily alight with genius – not that the Tsetse
> [T. S. Eliot] hadn't manifested something of the
> same thing to be sure – controlling it moreover to
> better purpose – but in Hambo [Lowry] it had been
> the more moving, and convincing, and alive, for its
> very uncontrolledness, its spontaneity and gay reck-
> lessness, not to mention its infectious gleeful delight in
> itself . . . life itself was a picnic of genius in which
> everyone could share. (*Ushant*, 1951, p. 269)

Yet this was accompanied by a ruthless literary pillage:

> And hadn't dear Hambo himself, and early, avowed his
> intention of absorbing all he jolly well could of D.
> [Aiken], and in that curious and ambivalent relation-
> ship of theirs, as of father and son, on one hand, and
> teacher and disciple on the other, absorbing him even
> to the point of annihilation? (p. 294)

The effect of Aiken's own novel, an attempt to 'eat'
Hambo before he is eaten, was eloquently described as
'underground bleeding' by Lowry – a phrase borrowed
from Aiken – to the young David Markson who twenty
years later had become his own spiritual 'son'.[8]
There is wide concurrence with Aiken's portrait: 'en-
gaging and volatile and unpredictable' are terms echoed
by schoolmates at the Leys, by Cambridge friends, by
a man with whom Lowry lodged in Vancouver.[9] He was
liable to gusts of rage – early instances of real violence
are recorded – or elation or despair. His drinking bouts
were sudden and obliterating; his open, variable temperament matches the open, variable style of his books,
where irony and humour play over tragic eloquence,
and where the angle of vision constantly changes. This
mercurial temperament found its best adjustment in
weaving fictions, which while containing a historic element, blended different times and places with the
imaginary life of books and authors; that, for Lowry, provided a secondary ballast. The historic base of his novels
was always extended into fantasy.
He would apply the same keen self-diagnosis to his
books and his life: 'My own worst fault in the past has
been precisely lack of integrity, and that is particularly
hard to face in one's own work. Youth, plus booze, plus
hysterical identification, plus self-deception, plus no work,

plus more booze' (*Letters*, p. 64). He detested 'clever' psychological reductive explanations; imaginative memory could completely absorb the historic past. The first voyage began Lowry's outer severance from his family and childhood, completed five years later; childhood events were darkened in memory until they seemed pure evil, whilst the distanced landscapes of home took on paradisal colouring. (Later, hell for Lowry became located in adolescence.)

The severance, leaving his past as dead, also left his imagination free to zoom in upon it. Some verses which he wrote in a very dark period of exile in Mexico have been accepted by some writers on Lowry as fact:

An autopsy on this childhood then reveals
That he was flayed at seven, crucified at eleven,
And he was blind besides and jeered at
For his blindness.

At seven the young Lowry left home for prep. school: the 'flaying' and 'crucifixion' represent the ordeals of school life (see below p. 110). The 'blindness' was a relatively bad attack of corneal ulceration, and while Lowry believed that as the result of neglect it lasted about four years[10] and that he was not allowed home because of his disfigurement, his family affirm that it lasted only a few weeks; his father at once arranged for a consultant, Dr Hudson, to see Malcolm and their family photographs of this period show him happily on vacation (I have seen these, taken at ages 10–15). Another dream-memory blew up what was perhaps the recollection of a nursemaid tucking him tightly into a pram against the winds that blow on the high sandstone bluff where his first home stood, into a threat of murder, from which he was saved by his elder brother![11] (Later, in the 1930s he believed his family set male nurses quietly to spy on him.)

His brothers think that Malcolm was a normally happy child; his brilliant record at golf, and his very good tennis prove that he was neither blind nor lame. Physically he was tougher than his next brother, Russell. The incommunicable panics of childhood when recalled feel as if they lasted for years; intensity of feeling has become duration, 'on the hearthrug gazing into hell'.[12]

The same brother remembers that at a birthday party around 1930, Lowry's father, after proposing his health in 'Mr Whiteway's admirable but not very stimulating cider' asked Malcolm for his earliest recollection:

> Malcolm frowned across the table at me, then looked up at the ceiling and said – and I really do quote: 'As far as I can remember my childhood was one of perpetual gloom. I was either blind, constipated or a cripple. In later years my only pleasurable experience was sneaking off occasionally with Russell to the pictures.' Period. You can imagine this dropped on the room like the second Ice Age. It certainly photographed itself on my memory. Nothing happened. Father cleared his throat and we moved on to the pudd.[13]

Malcolm spent the rest of his life looking for a substitute family group: he found one among the fishermen of Dollarton, British Columbia (in fantasy, his later heroes were intermarried with this group). The pain of leaving this little 'family' led to the revival of buried memories of earlier groups; but he never ceased to mourn Dollarton.

Malcolm was not, as he once averred, born into a huntin' and shootin' family; nor was he descended as he claimed from Robert the Bruce, nor from a Norwegian sea-captain. To his Canadian friends he enlarged the grandeur of his original family and their exploits, as he also magnified his own; his grandfather is met on all seven seas, usually going down with his ship and once ordering her to be sunk by gunfire because of cholera on board!

The fantasy of Norwegian ancestry came from Lowry's total indentification with Nordahl Grieg, and Grieg's novel of a seafarer's first voyage, *Skibet gaar videre* (1927), which underpinned Lowry's own first work.[14] The story of this largely imaginary relation with Grieg formed the subject of another work, lost in the fire that destroyed his cabin at Dollarton in June 1944; to the end of his life Lowry was trying to turn Grieg's novel into a play. The Norwegian name Sigbjørn Wilderness commemorates this identification. Elsewhere Lowry's jest about his own hated first name said he had been so christened by choice of his eldest brother Stuart, to commemorate the Clarence who drowned in the butt of Malmsey![15] Consequently, another of his characters became Bill Plantagenet. In later life he assumed his grandfather's name and called himself Malcolm Boden Lowry; he now attributed his odd gait to a gun battle in Penang on his first voyage (his elder brother was crippled in the foot in the First World War). Both in life and fiction a note of elation may be heard whenever Lowry claims for himself a seaman's instinct; this imaginative identification sustained his exile, when he lived in a beach hut built over the tidal waters of Vancouver Bay; it proved the strongest link between his experience and his reading.

The historic facts are that Lowry's father, a Liverpool cotton-broker, was a self-made man, who in his youth assumed exceptionally heavy family responsibilities for brothers, sisters and cousins.[16] The Lowry family, a tough, shrewd, humorous race, have produced accountants, civil servants, surgeons, agriculturalists. Arthur Lowry began as a Methodist, and having seen the effects of alcohol on some business acquaintance, he discouraged drinking in his home, together with smoking, parties and jazz. On the other hand, he was devoted to sport; at the top of the house where Malcolm was born he built a gymnasium; later, on his estate at Caldy, a Deeside village on the Wirral peninsula, he laid out a private golf course. He himself was awarded a medal for diving into the Mersey to rescue a bather in difficulties, during the course of his morning walk to the Liverpool ferry. As he moved up in the world, he gave generously to his sons of what he saw as the best – a public school education, lavish opportunities to excel at sport – while keeping a tight paternalistic financial control. The little band of brothers became expert at out-flanking paternal fiats; after serving in the First World War, the eldest married and escaped to Texas. The three remaining boys were left much to themselves since Mrs Lowry took little part in the boys' daily lives, except to preside at meals, Wilfrid acting as 'nanny' to the other two. (Mrs Lowry was 36 when she produced Malcolm; troubles of her menopause would come during his childhood.)

Born Evelyn Boden, she was the daughter of a Liverpool sea-captain, commander of a four-masted vessel, who about 1880 had died of cholera on the homeward voyage from Calcutta. His vessel, then commanded by the first officer, spoke another vessel, and gave this news, but subsequently vanished, and was presumed lost in a storm with all hands. Lowry's grandmother and his aunt told him tales of his grandfather and preserved the relics of old voyages; this, then, was the first alternative model to that of sport and conformity.[17]

Wilfrid, the second brother, taught the two youngsters to read, play games, ride bicycles, and frequent the cinema, where he would transport them, Russell on the carrier of his motorbike and Malcolm perched on the petrol tank! Four years after Wilfrid was capped for England at Rugby, Malcolm succeeded in winning a golf championship for boys under eighteen, held on the Royal Liverpool Links at Hoylake. But his next public game was catastrophic, after holing out in four, and he abruptly quitted the sport. At the same time, Wilfrid married, and the eldest brother returned from Texas – a Bohemian and exotic character, a talented artist and caricaturist who instead of Wilfrid's reading in Henty, Jeffrey Farnol and Ian Hay, offered Malcolm a diet of Eugene O'Neill, Cervantes, Balzac, Joyce. At his home the sixteen-year-old could smoke and drink and jest; to the end Stuart Lowry remained intermittently in contact. Malcolm's adolescence coincided with the transfer from identification with Wilfrid to identification with Stuart, the flamboyant traveller with his Texan shirts, his bar bells, and possibly a hint of that psychic sensitivity which developed from Malcolm's 'uncertain temper'. Malcolm's fluid and mobile instability of mood may have developed psychic flashes of telepathy and clairvoyance.[18]

The later stories about his childhood which Malcolm recounted show a clear pattern of displacement. He turned his mother's illness and her consequent absences from home into a tale that *he* was the sufferer, *he* was banished. To be separated from the mother can produce moods of dissociation, and even splitting of personality.[19] As the youngest of the family, Malcolm would be the most heavily exposed to psychological distress by his mother's illness. He spent his life looking for substitute mothers; his wife fulfilled this role, eventually, even to the extent of showing him how to dress himself; in bad moments he accused her of making him a child substitute.

A 'screen memory' as Day terms it, made him think he had been introduced at the age of five to the effects of venereal disease by his eldest brother taking him to the Anatomical Museum in Paradise Street, Liverpool (also the site of the 'Flying Angel' H.Q. of merchant navy welfare). This fantasy covers the origin of deep-seated fear. In fact Stuart Lowry was probably not around at the time because he was in the army.

Russell Lowry has described Malcolm's infant rages, which led him to hurl at his brother such objects as a spoonful of porridge, a plate of rice pudding or a silver sugar sifter. Wilfrid asserts that once Malcolm picked up Russell and threw him fully dressed, into a bath. Russell adds:

> Maybe indeed these infant rages were later distilled into bursts of energy and a scattered range of enthusiasms for such diverse things as hymn tunes, footpaths, long words which he couldn't pronounce, stamps, the theatre, the ukelele (we spent untold cheery hours making up execrable songs . . . 'I'll take my Alice to the Crystal Palace at the end of the Chinese War' comes back to me still), and many many more . . . He never seemed to be going anywhere definite in those days . . . He gradually moved into the world of the bizarre. Liked it. Found it worked as far as he was concerned . . . He was a charming, kind, generous, and infinitely amusing person – and by ordinary conventional standards – as mad as a hatter . . . He enjoyed it and felt he was cocking a snook at life. He just loved being bizarre. A much maligned father always paid the bills.

Finally Russell Lowry indulges in his own fantasy

> I have come to a feeling that some day Malcolm and I

will meet – perhaps under a by then long extinct
volcano. 'Why, Russ', he'll say, 'It's you: have some of
this excellent Holy Spirit. They damn it, specially for
me, on Saints' Days' . . . and we shall laugh.

Malcolm was to quarrel finally with Russell in a tremendous drunken scene at home – to quarrel, in Russell's
phrase 'à outrance'. But Wilfrid wrote occasionally to his
younger brother and Stuart more frequently. Malcolm's
visit to Europe in 1948–9 was spent on the continent,
with only a few hours' drinking at London airport in tran-
sit on return.

The family still went on being active in Malcolm's
imagination – in the latest years he was writing about
them in short stories – but in life their ways had parted,
essentially in adolescence, finally in 1932.

Mutations came at a deep level. It was easier to develop
nonconformist traits at school than at home; drink was an
obvious way of defying his puritanical and abstemious
father. Malcolm also began to use his pen in scathing
reports of school games, drawing cries of protest from his
schoolmates.[20] At the same time, he began to publish
short stories and verses, learnt to play the taropatch (a
small ukelele) by ear, and to compose with his friend
Ronnie Hill, the future band leader, with whom he spent
long sessions in the music room. In the spring of 1926 he
succeeded also, thanks to Wilfrid, in getting a trip
abroad.[21]

After his eastern voyage, Lowry went for a term
(December 1927–March 1928) to a college at Bonn, then
stayed in London till his voyage to the West Indies and
New England (May–September 1929).

For Lowry, Cambridge university proved only a return
to the cage, much resented; for the mutations were irre-
versible. His family saw him little; after 1932, even less.

At first his father paid an allowance; in 1938 he set up a special trust, but forbade family communication, although Malcolm continued to write to 'my dear darling precious little mother' – with nothing to say. Arthur Lowry died in February 1945, not as Malcolm was wont to assert of cirrhosis of the liver,[22] but of carcinoma of the rectum; Wilfrid, breaking silence, wrote about the war, the bombing of Merseyside, and his father's death, only to be answered with a letter about a football match, which upset him so much that he did not write again; yet Malcolm magnified his brother's war service mockingly.[23] Stuart Lowry crossed to France in the spring of 1949, where according to the family, Malcolm, who had come back for a holiday, was in trouble with the police and in danger of jail (cf. Day, pp. 402–3). With Margerie, he arranged for Malcolm to go to hospital in Paris, and settled some debts. But when the Lowrys returned to England in 1954, there was no contact, until on 28 June 1957 the Hailsham police telephoned, asking for Lowry's next-of-kin. Wilfrid replied that Mrs Margerie Lowry if available was next-of-kin, and rang Stuart who was on holiday abroad but returned to go to the funeral (Day, p. 54).

Rifts of such dimensions suggest that the link to be broken was strong. Social elevation had spelt constriction; the unfamiliar pattern of boarding school enclosed the little group. (All went to the Leys School, Cambridge.) Malcolm hated this exile. Mr and Mrs Lowry, starting in New Brighton close to the Methodist church, moved in 1906 to a relatively modest but substantial villa, where Malcolm was born. It stands on the very highest point of the red sandstone ridge overlooking fifteen golf courses, four light-houses, the sand-dunes and market gardens of the Wirral Peninsula. This region is the setting of the home scenes of Lowry's first novel, and he seems to know it street by street. He reverts to it in one of his

latest tales, 'Ghostkeeper'. The newly built piece of
stockbrokers' Tudor at Caldy to which the family
moved in 1910 overlooked the Dee estuary and the Clwyd
mountain range. Cut off from their old church (and
moving towards the Church of England), the Lowrys lost
some social contacts; others came through sport, or such
extraordinary treats as a visit which in the summer of 1918
Arthur Lowry arranged for his boys to see a 'Q' ship in
Liverpool Bay.

Malcolm kept that event for later use. A paradisal
memory of the 'primal' landscape of home remained,
quite detached from the memory of events. One local
family, children of a poet, were used as models in *Under
the Volcano* for the hard-drinking Taskersons amongst
whom the hero appears as an orphan. The Wibberlie
Wobberlie Song, which in that novel the young Geoffrey
sings with Laruelle, a song about getting drunk and
ogling the girls, had been in real life a gesture of defiance
towards father, as well as having the practical use that
Lowry acknowledged – 'the traditional song of all our
family that all the Lowry brothers sang at a certain ordeal
for new boys at school ... I am not at all sure that the
composer was not my eldest brother himself.'[24]

To stand on the site of either of Lowry's homes is to
look westward over a wide scene of great beauty and
variety. Behind, and eastward, across the Mersey estuary
lies the port of Liverpool, which for Lowry came to
symbolise hell; before, the expanse of the Bay. Green
levels behind the dunes stretch towards the Clwyd range;
the sunsets are of an extraordinary brilliance. This was
Lowry's first Eden.

The topography of Leasowe lighthouse, the sunken
remains of the primeval forest in the early golfing scenes
of *Under the Volcano* are all faithful, though the scene
is not placed on those links where Lowry played.[25] The

bunkers on the golf courses were well known as courting places, where village children delighted to make rude incursions on these forlorn attempts at privacy, as Laruelle intrudes on Geoffrey.

When in Mexico Geoffrey Firmin stands upon the *mirador* of Laruelle's house, looking out over the ravine, he sees – as if with a zooming camera shot – across time and space; the ravine turns into the 'Golgotha Bunker':

> It was as if they were standing on a lofty golf tee some-
> where. High up, an eagle drove downwind in one[26] ...
> and on that other side what strange fairways could
> be contrived, crossed by lone railway lines ... over the
> hills and far away, like youth itself, like life itself ...
> to the Farolito, the nineteenth hole. (p. 207)

He looks back to the self who had 'once enjoyed such a simple, healthy stupid good thing as golf' and becomes in mind 'a Donne of the fairways', recalling in a parody of *Hymn to God my God in my sickness* the exact catastrophe ('holing out in four') which had decided young Lowry to abandon this path to fame for life:

> Who holds the flag while I hole out in three? Who
> hunts my Zodiac Zone along the shore? And who,
> upon the last and final green, though I hole out in four,
> accepts my ten and three score ... Though I have
> more. (p. 207)

October Ferry holds a companion scene, where the Zodiac Zone (an old type of golf ball) is found. The burnt ancestral home of the hero is to be rebuilt,[27] and the rebuilding is tenderly described in terms of an oriole's nest which is seen tossing beside a lake in the breeze that bears over a deserted golf course, with the scent of the grass, the smell of charred wood. Like the ghosts of

31

Cathy and Heathcliff returning in *Wuthering Heights* to their Yorkshire moors, the lovers are set in a scene composed of Wirral – its moths, heathers and harebells – and other places. A translucent invocation of the past joins with a future challenging but not hopeless:

> and now the windy whistling empty golf links themselves with their blowing spiny spring grasses and sand dunes and stricken stunted thorn bushes like *Wuthering Heights* 'I lingered round them, under that benign sky, watching the moths fluttering among the harebells' – the course! – but ah! what further hazards lurked before them there, what roughs and bunkers and traps and dog-legged approaches and dongas and treacherous blind (and nineteenth!) holes and final, it was to be hoped too, bright fairways ... (*October Ferry*, pp. 112–13)

One of the catastrophes of addiction is that it prevents the growth of personality, which tends to become fixed at some point in the past. Lowry grew through his work. From childhood it had been hard for him to work to time; in his books time is all-important. Especially in this last book, by continuous integration the past and present are woven together in a single image, with an effect like that of an Elizabethan tragic pun, or an 'echo' in Monteverdi. This danger had been diagnosed in *Under the Volcano*, where to his younger brother Geoffrey Firmin looked 'as if fate had fixed his age at some unidentifiable moment in the past, when his persistent objective self, perhaps weary of standing askance and watching his downfall, had at last withdrawn from him altogether, like a ship secretly leaving the harbour at night' (p. 187).[28]

Since there are no words for the 'inenarrable incon-

ceivable desolate sense of having no right to be where
you are; the billows of inexhaustible anguish haunted by
the insatiable albatross of self' (*Hear Us O Lord*, p. 31)
the struggle inexorably takes the form of reconciling
the warring self and the outer world. 'Personal responsibility is complete, though the life is all interior' (*Dark
as the Grave*, p. 239). Through a dream world of fiction
it is possible to 'make his acceptance of that other world
you think so highly of' (*Lunar Caustic*, p. 58). Thus the
present time is redeemed.

Under the Volcano first created such a complete world
of time and a mythology. The difference between that
novel and the later torsos may be suggested by comparing
Blake's early lyrics and his Prophetic Books. The lyrics are
the more fully formed, but the Prophetic Books in their
traditional yet personal use of symbolic material can be
entered only by a degree of sympathetic identification.
Yet this is not a private world. Lowry's later work calls
for the same patient editing, to build up the total effect
upon which he had laid such stress; his mythology derived
from many books, but likewise from his own personal
experience. Out of his own life he built a set of personal
conventions, within which frame his work grew; and
these conventions, though related to such general theory
as the cabbalistic or Neo-Platonic, illuminate the purpose,
though of course this can be done successfully at some
times, feebly at others.

In the later works, a cosmic landscape of heaven and
hell emerges, as Lowry went on to write what he termed
'Under *Under the Volcano*' – books darker in tone, without the humour and balance of that shapely and yet
molten, riotously absurd and horrific masterpiece. An
editor has expressed astonishment that Lowry spent five
years on anything as unformed as *Dark as the Grave*;
Lowry has pleaded that these writings, some of which

are very fragmentary, show 'only the battering the human spirit takes (doubtless because it is overreaching itself) in its ascent towards its true purpose' (*Letters*, p. 63).[29] Because they are open and unformed they can be inclusive.

The paradisal vision is achieved in the last short story of *Hear Us O Lord* (designed as the conclusion of the whole series of Lowry's books). As part of a tragic vision, it is recovered by renunciation in *October Ferry*, of which Lowry said 'It isn't a "good" book. It doesn't aim to be. It thinks of itself as a classic (especially and/or in conjunction with its fellows)' (*Letters*, p. 360). Among proofs of balance his recovered sense of humour, again at once both riotous and horrifically absurd, here becomes structurally predominant.

The name of paradise is Eridanus.

It appears – though not with that name – in *Under the Volcano*, for Yvonne, Hugh and finally the Consul see a vision of the Canadian paradise.[30] Mexico is hell; the volcanoes and the vultures and pariah dogs need no annotation; the ruined palace of Maximilian and more mysterious Aztec history reflect the derelict and deposed indignity of the ex-Consul:

> I sometimes think of myself as a great explorer who
> has discovered some extraordinary land from which he
> can never return to give his knowledge to the world;
> but the name of this land is hell.
>   It is not Mexico, of course, but in the heart.
> (Under the Volcano, pp. 41–2)

But 'through hell there is a path', and in dreams he has seen the northern paradise of mountains and blue water; in the last half hour of his life, he sees behind the bed in the brothel a calendar set to the future,[31] showing the Canadian scene of Dollarton.

Eridanus, river of youth and river of death, raised to a constellation in the heavens but in its chthonic aspect the Styx, is also the river in which Phaethon, the over-weening son of Apollo was drowned as he attempted to guide the horses of the sun. It is also the River Po, at the mouth of which, in Ravenna, lies the tomb of Dante, upon whose great trilogy Lowry sometimes modelled his structure. It is therefore much more than the imaginative name given to the actual Dollarton, B.C., supposedly after a wrecked ship found there, beached, with its name and port of origin on the stern: *Eridanus*, Liverpool – 'seem-ing to comment on my own source, for I too had been born in that terrible city whose main street is the ocean' (*Hear Us O Lord*, p. 225). Floating just below the surface in deep water so clear that the name was visible, a sunken derelict canoe named *Intermezzo* also seemed to be a relic of two lovers (p. 230); and floating under the surface of the magnificent images of Van-couver Bay is a mirror image of the shore Lowry knew as a child.

In the great harbour at Vancouver, Lowry looked east to the city and all its Dantesque horrors ('Beneath the Malebolge lies Hastings Street') with Port Burnaby, here renamed Port Boden, on the opposite shore. The Shell refinery, by an imperfection of neon lighting, sometimes appeared as hell. The great mountains of Indian Arm, closing the Canadian scene on the other side, are perhaps no grander than to a child's imagination had seemed the Clwyd range.[32]

A number of unpublished poems deal directly with this childhood Eden; one was written at Dollarton, during the second world war, as a lament for a lost Eden, looking westward.

35

Epitaph for our Gardener, dead near Liverpool.
. . . Good folk of Wirral
Empty the sky one instant of evil,
And then look far to sea – you did not know
Lycidas died out there, beyond Hilbre . . .
But in Flintshire still great furnaces glow,
And now the world our garden is, of iron,
Remember him to whom it was not so . . .
Here lies more than a man, here lies an age.

Half a century ago, the Wirral was still a strange mixture of countryside untouched but surrounded and en-
croached on by urban life – little pockets of market
gardening or farming behind the windswept dunes, fine
old houses of great Liverpool merchants near tiny wind-
ing village streets, with the local council busy changing
Jockey Lane into Sandcliffe Road. The mixture and super-
imposition of totally different strata could not last – and
by now the motorway has obliterated what Lowry
knew – yet this primal landscape fitted well with what
he saw in Canada, the advance of despoilment upon a
rural scene.

In that idyll and hymn to wedlock 'The Forest Path to
the Spring', with its companion piece 'The Bravest Boat',
a trustful release into play, the freedom to recover a
childish self comes from a happy marriage.[33] In the
second, a childish ritual is gravely re-enacted; in the first,
the mysterious lengthening and shortening of the path
and the fantastic fear that in its course one might dis-
appear, are part of a deeper ritual of recovery. The path
is reached by means of a rotten old ladder salvaged from
the sea, which is 'the past, up and down which one's mind
every night meaninglessly climbs' (*Hear Us O Lord*,
p. 261; cf. *Selected Poems*, p. 69 for a poetic version of
this same passage).

Another piece of salvage, the canister which is daily carried along the forest path to the spring and which mysteriously grows heavier or lighter carries a memory of sharp guilt and failure from Lowry's first voyage – here transformed by the benign rose-colour of fiction. The teller of the tale recognises this canister as the kind he had seen on English ships as a filter when he was a fireman, and thinks it smells of lime juice, which is so strong that as well as for drinking it is used for deck scrubbing. So he makes up a little tale to amuse his wife about a 'green' mess boy who had put in too much lime juice, corroded the metal, the bosun had come off duty thirsty, drunk the rusty liquid, torn the filter off the wall, threatened to 'crown' the unlucky mess boy and thrown it overboard (*Hear Us O Lord*, p. 240).

The original fact is preserved in a letter of one of Lowry's shipmates.[34] On his first voyage, the bosun's boy 'Lobs' Lowry had poured undiluted lime juice into the mess-room filter. This became corroded and the lining peeled off; the resulting 'devil's brew' 'nearly lost the lives of several members of the crew ... The cleaning-out filter job that Lobs earned for himself was very little to pay for what may have been tragedy.' Just as memory blackened his childhood, so here it gilds the past, gently 'misrepresenting the very events of his life for the sake of making them into a bearable pattern' (*October Ferry*, p. 210).

The scale of the landscape at Dollarton reduced earlier scenes to Lilliputian size, and their sorrows likewise; it is heroic yet domestic: 'Sometimes in the early mornings the mist looked like a huge family wash the property of Titans, hanging out to dry between the folds of their lower hills. At other times all was chaos, and Valkyries of storm drift drove them out of the ever receding heaven' (*Hear Us O Lord*, p. 215).

Between the mountains and the cabin, the great tidal waters flowed in complex currents and cross settings, neither sea nor river but partaking of both: 'mysterious and multiform in its motion, and in the mind as the mind flowed with it'. Lowry's style itself reflects the changing mist and fog and wind, the shifting waters and the comings and goings of birds. His fluid movement, with the successive layers of symbolic depth, gives a two-way rip-tide movement and the characters 'were not looking at the view, but at something in themselves, or that had been in themselves' (*October Ferry*, p. 250). The path to the spring through the woods was called the Bell–Proteus path.[35] The Protean qualities of this majestic scene passed into Lowry's language, the shot-silk of his evocative descriptions: he offered in his work something made from his life, 'The Flowers of the Past'. Exile is a form of suicide that may become rebirth.

> There is no poetry when you live there,
> Those stones are yours, those noises are your mind.
> The forging thunderous trams and streets that bind
> You to the dreamed-of bar where sits despair
> Are trams and streets; poetry is otherwise . . .
> But move you towards New Zealand or the Pole,
> Those stones will blossom and the noises sing . . .
> *Selected Poems*, p. 16

From the first stages of his journey to the last, Lowry transformed his inner explorations; accepting change, he bound with words the past and present.[36] Even Eridanus is not the final paradise, though far further on the journey than the primal Eden. 'Perhaps it's something like a sunrise: when it's at its very best you say, oh if it would just stay like that forever, but if it did you'd never know what full noon was like, or midnight either. No, it was

38

time to leave, however much it hurts . . .' (*October Ferry*, p. 325). To accept change is not to accept inconstancy, although, in the end, it is to accept death, the dark passage of Charon's ferry.

2

Outward Bound from Liverpool
(*Ultramarine*, 1933)

Malcolm Lowry's first novel traces his first voyage; all that follow are cast in the form of exile and journeying, by more ships, buses, planes: the search of the evicted for a home; this design-governing posture, as he would have termed it, linked him later to a leading theme of Canadian writing.[1] *Ultramarine*, revised a little, formed the opening in a sequence of his works to be named *The Voyage that Never Ends*, where the early experiences reappear in varied forms; in *Under the Volcano*, its course is attributed to that of the life of Hugh Firmin; in 'Elephant and Colosseum' – heroic and magnified – of Kennish Drumgold Cosnahan.

Initiation into the life of a cabin-boy led into the further ordeals of the addict, the artist, the visionary, and remained as a constellation in Lowry's mind, joined to the memory of his grandfather, therefore joined to his childhood; joined also to his brother's discovery, O'Neill; joined finally with the fishermen of Dollarton, especially the Manxman, Jimmy Craige.[2] In the sailor's rôle he found a shaping identity, in a society simpler and closer than any ashore, to which he clung all his life. The rhythm of his stories is the rhythm of a voyage – a slow even monotone, with all the action crowded at the end; his build-up is protracted, his endings always sharp and decisive.

When Lowry shipped in *s.s. Pyrrhus*, Captain Elford, outward bound from Liverpool on 14 May 1927 for

40

eastern ports, this voyage lasted less than six months, but he took two subsequently to America and Norway. The raw experience was shaped by two books of the sea which both appeared in 1927 – Conrad Aiken's *Blue Voyage* and Nordahl Grieg's *Skibet gaar videre* (*The Ship Sails On*). The American poet and novelist Aiken played an important and direct part in Lowry's life; yet the impress of Grieg's work is the stronger, although less personal.

The name of Lowry's first hero, Eugene Dana Hilliot, evokes Eugene O'Neill and Charles Dana, seafaring by steam and sail; and twenty years later Lowry wrote to a young admirer who had become 'possessed' by *Under the Volcano*, that such identification is above all creative, impelling the young writer on; he cites Keats's identification with Chatterton, Aiken's with T. S. Eliot and Eliot's with Laforgue.[3] Powerful, though largely unrecognised, such identification is perhaps religious in origin 'or something to do with evolution'.

Ultramarine was crammed with as much experience as he could muster, nonetheless; from his stay in Bonn he drew the portrait of the German wireless operator. Hilliot's Cambridge career is freely adapted from Lowry's own.[4] The schoolgirl golfer Janet Rohtraut Trevena who focuses Hilliot's dreams and hopes is cut out in *Under the Volcano* where England was Hugh Firmin's dream. 'He certainly didn't think of any other mistresses he might have had at home. His one or two affairs, if serious at the time, had been forgotten long ago' – he is altogether more sophisticated.

Hilliot is provided with a firm Freudian basis for going to sea; in his nursery hung a portrait of his mother's father. 'Why are you so dirty, Dana? My father was always so clean, so spruce. He had his Master's certificate before he was twenty-three! . . . He was an angel from heaven. He was bringing me a cockatoo' (pp. 118–19). In memory Hilliot's home scene is traversed again and again. The names are charged with their own incommunicable power, implacably particular, the seaman's rosary of his homesickness. Walks along the sea-front from New Brighton Tower to Egremont Ferry, walks on the Wirral, bus rides through the Birkenhead docks, the very names of the big yellow buses fill the void of days at sea. Janet has also been in Alesund, home of Hilliot's ancestors, while in the central chapter, the drunken confessional scene (chapter III), it is the topography of Cambridge that is recalled as Hilliot assumes a series of dream rôles – familial, literary, fantastic – to build a cosmic triumph where 'the important point is that the apparent facts are largely imaginary' (*Ultramarine*, p. 102). Hilliot recites to a German sailor all his ports of call; the voyage itself was a 'self inflicted penance' (p. 99), assumed to control this inner chaos; thus, by a magic recall of interior and exterior voyaging, the inrush of experience overwhelming a youthful mind is given shape. The words are picked up from everywhere and anywhere. 'But words, beyond the life of ships, dream on.' The two driving impulses are the dream of heroic exploit (rescuing the captive bird) and the dream of murdering an enemy (the cook, Andy). These two episodes had already appeared separately in the Cambridge magazine *Experiment*. In view of the hostile portrait of the homosexual quartermaster in *Ultramarine*, it is worth quoting Lowry's shipmate: 'He sorely disliked the old Q.M. who could read him like a book, in fact he averred he would write an article on this man but was told very forcibly that if he did so, a similar article would be written against himself.'

In 1928, Lowry's fan letter to Conrad Aiken about *Blue Voyage* was filled with quotation, ending with the thud of the engines, as did Aiken's own book – 'te-thrum-te-thrum-' but Lowry was most gripped by the poetic landscape, the hot white sand dunes with 'small yellow flowers, sapless and squat and spiny'. It is like his own landscape.

Blue Voyage tells of the passengers in an Atlantic crossing; its relation to Lowry's voyage is slight, but in the summer of 1929 Lowry crossed the Atlantic to be with Aiken, offered him 'filial affection' and allowed him at least a component part in the ambiguous father figure of *Ultramarine*. Aiken told of his 'first arrival in Cambridge, Mass., with broken suitcase and dirty socks and a taropatch and the much-thumbed blue-covered exercise book in which were the neatly pencilled first fragments of *Aquamarine*' (*Ushant*, 1953, p. 294). After an 'all but fatal wrestling match for the porcelain lid of the W.C.' that marked the beginnings, the charming 'Hambo' drifted around, playing his taropatch ('Aint got no money, Aint got a cent, Aint got a House, Cant pay the rent') but felt so free to act the magpie that Aiken marked up a copy of *Ultramarine* with *C.A.* against his own contributions.[5] Lowry spent his long vacations in Aiken's house at Rye, his father having thankfully accepted the transference of responsibility; it was to this region that Lowry returned when at last in 1954 he came back to a small village, Ripe, near Lewes.

His exile had begun in 1932, in Aiken's company; on a voyage to Spain, they discussed the construction of the novel Aiken was to write, an 'ambiguous book' breaking down reality into 'its so many and deceptive levels', as of a thousand-year-old palimpsest. It was to be 'a projection on a larger scale of all that had been implied in that view of the human psyche as an indecipherable or nameless land, a land of which one could make oneself the possessor by a mere strictness' (*Ushant*, pp. 322–5). A pattern for the design was worked out with the level of the actual succeeded by the level of the writer and again by the level of the novel-as-it-was-to-exist, which in turn had three levels: this is *Ushant* itself.

In Spain, later in Mexico, and later still in the depths of his misery in 1940, when Lowry was living in a kind of protective custody in Vancouver,[6] he turned to Aiken, who has testified to 'a quite astonishing pitch of divination – and a kind of co-operative and hallucinatory, alcoholic brilliance of statement unique in his experience' (*Ushant*, p. 229); Lowry agrees that the electric personal contact was an 'operation of the daimon' (*Letters*, p. 253) which he does not feel able to discuss.

Aiken suffered from some curious mental 'Rhythms' as he called them when he suddenly felt distanced from his surroundings. He knew that at such times, till his excellent 'machine' recovered its balance, he must keep himself cut off from other people. He was a little ruffled by Lowry's appropriation of the historic figure of William Blackstone for *Under the Volcano*. (Blackstone was an early Puritan emigrant from Cambridge to New England, who went to live among the Indians. Aiken had used him in his poem *The Kid*.)

To the end *Blue Voyage* remained part of the furniture of Lowry's mind; three examples will suffice. The striking phrase that records the hero's entry to the mental hospital in *Lunar Caustic*, 'with the dithering crack of a ship going on the rocks, the door shut behind him' (p. 11) is Aiken's; in *Under the Volcano*, the Consul says of a little cat 'She thinks I'm a tree with a bird in it' – a phrase which Aiken saw Lowry jot down! – and in *October Ferry*, a brisk exchange about marriage includes the two ironic ejaculations 'Merry laughter!' and 'Fire cannon and blow up ship!' (p. 103) originally associated by Aiken.[7]

One of the earliest parts of *Ultramarine*, for it first appeared in the Cambridge magazine *Experiment* under

the title 'At Port Swettenham', records an actual incident
in Lowry's first voyage, independently reported by his
shipmate, when the cabin-boy lacks the nerve to jump
into the water and rescue a pet bird; this is contrasted
with the original bravery of another seaman in climbing
the mast to bring down the wounded bird, a feat that is
related to a boyhood exploit of Aiken.[8]

The very title *Ultramarine* is of course an adaptation of
Blue Voyage – or a challenge to it – as an alternative,
later, *Purple Passage* seemed more appropriate! But in
general, *Ultramarine* is indebted to Aiken for verbal
patterns, whilst the larger structural pattern is indebted to
Grieg.

Another tale from the book *Ultramarine* was so far indebted to Nordahl Grieg as to carry the same title as his
book; in *Experiment*, no. 7, Lowry supplied under the
title 'Punctum indifferens; Skibet gaar videre' the story
of the quarrel with Andy, the Norwegian cook which
forms chapter IV of *Ultramarine*. It closely parallels the
fantasy of the hero of Grieg's book, that he is guilty of
murdering the fireman Anton.[9] Other incidents that echo
from Grieg to Lowry are the non-arrival of a letter for the
hero and its subsequent recovery, the decision to send him
down below to act as fireman – the culminating ordeal
for two heroes who are both sailing 'for experience' and
thereby find their relations with their shipmates made
difficult. Finally, Hilliot's ship was originally Norwegian
and is still covered with signs and instructions in Norwegian, which are given in full in the text.

The Ship Sails On (*Skibet gaar videre*) tells of the
voyage of the *Mignon*, a brute of a ship, in ballast from
Norway to South Shields, and thence to the Cape with
coal. Benjamin Hill joins her to find the forecastle full of
merry-making whores; at the end of the voyage, a stray
dog in his arms, he climbs the ship's rails for a suicide

bid; but both the hero and his dog are reprieved to face whatever further ordeals the voyage imposes.

Already the crew have driven through a storm; 'crowned' the steward with a dish of burnt porridge; one man leaves the ship to try prospecting for gold; another jumps ship after he has failed to rescue a child who fell into the dock; one syphilis case is left behind in hospital; there is a general fight; the fireman Anton is killed by falling off the stokehold ladder. All then feel remorse, for Anton had been jeered at because he would not join in complaints. Benjamin feels the guilt of an imaginary murder; 'he had murdered Anton every time he refused to show him kindness, every time he denied him':

> No questioning here; thought and reason were brought up short. Here it was only a presentiment, a vague dread that raised its pale and terrible face out of the mists, whispering 'There is no escape, Benjamin, and you know it – it is not sorrow you feel for this dead man, it is the remorse of one who has had a mystical share in a murder. But how? Oh, the ways of life are dark, a mysterious force crouches within you and fills your soul with terror; reason stands still; what do we know?' (*The Ship Sails On*, p. 80)

This is a key passage for the understanding of Lowry's work; he quoted the last phrase as having been repeated to him by Grieg in amazement at the series of co-incidences, or, as he called them, examples of the Law of Series, that connected the two of them (*Letters*, p. 264).

Benjamin has a vision of how he pushed Anton – 'was it the spectre of a murder he had committed in another existence? He didn't know.' The vision rapidly expands to cosmic dimensions – once again this was in Lowry's later work to become essential to his most powerful scenes.[10] The incident seemed to Lowry to reflect the death of his friend Paul Fitte, and this coincidence probably explains his extraordinary identification with Grieg. 'The ship is like the earth and the earth has a thousand ships. And what is the earth but a star in the face of the night?' On another planet, a pair of lovers see a shooting star and think it a sign of luck 'but the shooting star was the earth going out' (p. 90).

Nordahl Grieg was no mystic. A nephew of the composer Edward Grieg, and seven years older than Lowry, he was an active political radical who visited Russia, though he could not accept Stalin's régime. When the Germans invaded Norway he became Norway's leading poet of the Resistance, joined the Norwegian Air Force, and was shot down in flames over Berlin on 2 December 1943. His clear, ironic, concentrated writing is at the opposite pole from Lowry's; Yeats might have termed him Lowry's Anti-self.

In *The Ship Sails On* Lowry found not only a hero who gave him a complete feeling of identification, but also a series of ordeals of proper magnitude. He wrote many letters to Grieg but never posted them; he told his own young disciple David Markson that this kind of relation involved clairvoyance 'as you have proved yourself' (*Letters*, pp. 261, 265). It is incontestable that Lowry borrowed heavily and directly from *The Ship Sails On*. In later years he betrayed some anxiety about possible accusations of plagiarism, proposing a set of notes to record his debts in expiation of 'an Elizabethan unscrupulousness in my evil youth' (*Letters*, p. 115). He may have been pleased to get some suggestions to liven up his voyage, especially its hardships, for in *Under the Volcano* Hugh, recounting the story mentions with disgust that he had been shipped on an exceptionally spruce, well-ordered ship, with cabins for the seamen, and that in many ports he was not allowed ashore. Such a provident plan may well have been devised with the Blue Funnel Line by Lowry's father.[11]

Lowry and Grieg met in 1931, and the story of this meeting became the theme of the lost novel *In Ballast to the White Sea*, begun in New York in 1934 and lost in the fire which consumed the cabin at Dollarton in 1944. The ghost of his book haunts the later works – Lowry always meant to rewrite it – and perhaps was finally exorcised in *October Ferry*.[12] The story began at Cambridge – 'a stormy love affair with an older woman, the risk of being sent down for pursuing it' – the encounter with the book which absorbs him, so that the hero ('I am by and large, more or less and with reservations, A') starts to neglect his studies, drinks like a fish, drives a Dostoievskian brother to suicide, finds his own work increasingly worthless, and feels drawn irresistibly to the stokehold, to the fire, to further ordeals (*Letters*, p. 261). The whole universe seems to work against him; but when, after a startling series of coincidences, he lands in Norway, and meets his 'author' all becomes resolved, he finds happiness and rebirth.

> In effect, both the life of the imagination and life itself have been saved by A's having finally listened to the promptings of his own spirit, and acted upon those promptings rather than the analytic reductions of reason, though it is reason too – by virtue of the great harmony within the soul – that has been saved. (*Letters*, p. 263)

The meeting with Grieg fed his fantasy and not his technique; sometimes too the coincidences, synchronisings, or Law of Series seem to have been a little improved in the telling.[13] The version of this meeting which Lowry gave to James Stern in Paris in 1933 is slightly different.[14]

It seems to have made much less impression on Grieg than on Lowry, whose name is not so much as mentioned by Grieg's official biographer. Lowry on the other hand, used Norwegian, of which he had a very elementary knowledge, especially when talking of ships, as a kind of *poésie concrète*, or cabbalistic language. Whatever the qualities of the lost book, which ran to a thousand pages, it was meant to provide the happy conclusion, the *Paradiso* to the trilogy as Lowry originally conceived it. Its successor, *October Ferry*, occupies that place in the end, however small the actual likeness between these two works.[15]

In 1934 Lowry married an American, Jan Gabrial, but his heavy drinking led to a separation. Next year he followed her to New York where he acquired the basis for the purgatorial part of his trilogy, the magnificent *Lunar Caustic*. Originally conceived in 1936, it was grounded on Lowry's own experience as committed mental patient in the Bellevue Hospital, New York, during 1935.[16]

Lowry recognised that this was a master-work, but meant to expand it; with it he found his true theme, and was out of his apprenticeship. The hero is a seaman, a jazz musician, a drunkard; and although he thinks as he awakes that he is still on shipboard, his voyage is arrested. Outside the hospital, ships pass on New York's East River. Gradually Sigbjørn Lawhill, or Bill Plantagenet, focused.[17]

Someone sat on his bed with a hand on his pulse and forcing his eyes open he saw a wavering white form which divided into three, became two and finally came into focus as a man in a white gown.

The man – a doctor? – dropped Plantagenet's wrist. 'You've certainly got the shakes' he said. (p. 18)

The doctor, an ambiguous figure, in the 'analytic reductions of reason' names Plantagenet Mr Remorse; he invariably supplies the dry, deflating retort. Plantagenet has come in proclaiming that he himself is a ship, addressing the doctor as 'father', and asserting that he is sent 'To save my father, to find my son, to heal the immedicable horror of opposites.'

The patients include an old man, Kalowsky the 'wandering Jew', and a child-murderer, a boy named Garry, who loves to tell stories:

> Wherever I am if I'm up in the air or under the sea, or in the mountains, anywhere I can tell a story. No matter where you put me, even in prison, I can be sitting, not sitting. Eating, not eating. I can put the the whole thing in a story, that's what makes it a story. (p. 15)

The third patient who emerges is a wild Negro, a ship's fireman named Battle whose jazz, dancing and frenzies supply all the energy of the first part of this tale. 'He's crazy, but you can't help liking him' says Garry, who teaches him to semaphore: ' "Move yo' lef' han' to E. To make M, move to F" Battle repeated after Garry, then immediately he started to shadow box again, though Garry went on signalling' (p. 25). In his long interview with Claggart, the doctor, Plantagenet accuses him of trying to adjust these patients to an impossibly distorted and corrupt city 'just as you might imagine wounded soldiers being patched up to be sent back to fight again by surgeons who had been smashed up themselves'. The psychology sounds nearer to R. D. Laing than to Freud or Jung. The 'uncomplaining acceptance of their own degeneration' marks Battle and the other hopeless ones; but Garry's stories with their symbols of disaster represent his craving for freedom, and in the doctor's desire to wean the boy from his fantasies, Plantagenet feels the creative act is insulted; 'all his stories are about things collapsing, falling apart... It extends to the world – that sense of decay, that necessity of blasting away the past, the feeling of *vertige...*' Through his dream world, the boy could 'make his acceptance of that world you think of so highly'.

There would appear to be a sense in which the doctor is justified in his constant attack on Plantagenet's views of the others 'Are you sure you're not talking about yourself?' Nevertheless this is not a solipsist's nightmare, although the description of Garry's stories could be applied pretty directly to *Under the Volcano*.

With Plantagenet himself 'drink is not the problem'; the horrors lie deeper. In so far as he retains his identity as seaman and jazz player (as for being a novelist, he would rather be a bacon scrubber, a watcher of manholes, wanderer under trains in stations to see that nobody is using the toilet!), he gives the doctor a message for Melville about Billy Budd, the handsome sailor, who though innocent is hanged. By doing it he casts the doctor for the rôle of villain – though in the earlier version, he was the protagonist's cousin and fellow worker – since 'Claggart', the doctor's name, is that of the evil petty officer in *Billy Budd*.

Within the tight shape of a *novella*, *Lunar Caustic* holds the density and depth of the later works, their direct vividness of talk and layers of poetic reverberation. In *Ultramarine*, the sailors' talk had been caught by Lowry's impeccable ear, but not built into a structure; sometimes the memory was irrelevant in the sense that it belonged only to his own past.[18] The ships that pass by the hospital, the derelict barge that represents the inmates, give way to a wider storm scene, the 'inevitable deluge' in which

violent and almost supernatural energy is loosed. Plantagenet watches from a barred window as lovers in the park
flee, the leaves are stripped from trees, the river sparkles
like ginger ale, and seethes with a million sequins. Plantagenet's thoughts flow past with the river, but they cannot
escape and always contract to the hospital, the point from
which he is watching. He watches a ship and sees a vision
of the ship on which with his bride he had sailed to Melville's New Bedford coast. Everything is still functioning
in degeneration. 'Metamorphosis nudged metamorphosis'
while a part of him stands outside and contemplates his
own storm.[19]

No less than four of Lowry's major works culminate in
a storm scene, and in each case it is man's total relation to
his environment which is imaged in this violence without
and within. The full orchestration of heaven and earth
still leaves the mind of Garry, the child-murderer, frozen;
purgatory is outside not inside the hospital. 'It only looks
like spring . . . the clover's growing slow, the dandelions
are not out quite, but they will be, and look, there's a
path running through the little grass hill. It only looks
like spring, that's all' (pp. 71–2). The connection with purgatory is made explicit in one of Lowry's unpublished
poems, *At Dollarton Bus Stop*:

> . . . It was stupid to be afraid,
> Since now we go to love and tea
> All merry as a marriage bell.
> And yet, it might be, one was dead,
> It might, our halt was purgatory,
> It might be now, heaven or hell
> It might, that view was not the sea.

The depths of the ordeal are plumbed in this demonic
storm. In one of his letters Lowry adapted from Dante an

image of the caryatids of anguish which defines Plantagenet's rôle:[20] 'I've been there before, brother – in fact, I'm there now – let me stand like a caryatid down there, while you step on my head and go round the other way' (*Letters*, p. 260).

Lowry's Tartarus
(*Under the Volcano*, 1946)

Compassion he valued above all things,
even though he saw the weakness in that desire
(*Hear Us O Lord*, p. 86)

The original short tale of *Under the Volcano* (chapter
vIII in the novel) is an ironic version of the tale of the
Good Samaritan, 'founded on experience' as Lowry declared. No one would help the wounded and dying Indian
found at the Mexican roadside, since under the law this
would make him an accomplice to the crime; from the
bus which passes by, one of the passengers descends to
rob the dying man. '*Pobrecito*' murmurs one bystander,
'*chingarn*' another; these two words, 'the one of compassion, the other of obscene contempt' cancel out.

As the bus rolls away the horrified young Englishman,
Hugh Firmin, who was witness to the inbred passivity of
the Mexican peasants applied a lesson he had been taught
at college: 'It was for them as if through the various
tragedies of Mexican history, pity the impulse to advance
and terror the impulse to retreat ... had been reconciled
finally by prudence, the conviction that it was better to
stay where you are.'[1] As he progresses through the twelve
hours of his pitiful and relentless last day, from drink to
drink, from *cantina* to *cantina*, Geoffrey Firmin the Consul
seems to call the whole universe into operation against
him; the mountain seems about to fall on him, the ravine
gaping to receive him. No Samaritan can help here:

Popocatepetl towered through the window, its immense
flanks partly hidden by rolling thunderheads; its peak

blocking the sky, it appeared almost right overhead, the *barranca*, the Farolito, directly beneath it. Under the volcano! It was not for nothing the ancients had placed Tartarus under Mt Aetna, nor within it, the monster Typhoeus . . .

(*Under the Volcano*, p. 340).

To a member of the Canadian Broadcasting Corporation, Lowry made the main points succinctly:[2] yes, there is a cosmic dimension: it all happens under Scorpio the sign of suicide; the political parable of civil war in Spain and the approach of war is there from the start. The Consul is Faustian; he has been a cabbalist, and because 'he might be a black magician', the very elements have turned against him. Not only is he evicted from the garden (the Garden of Eden) which he has helped to destroy but 'he has turned into a man that is all destruction – in fact he has almost ceased to be a man altogether, and his human feelings merely make things more agonising for him but don't alter things in the least; he is thus in hell'. He is inaccessible to his friends, as they are to him. As he is shot and flung, still alive, into the ravine, 'somebody threw a dead dog after him down the ravine'.

Lowry's intentions were more complex than a summary would imply. The story of a drunk is told with that 'hallucinatory, alcoholic brilliance' that Aiken noted. Parts of it are comic. It can be read simply as a story – not very easily, however – offering an 'open myth'. Lowry accepted interpretations he had not considered himself; he was ready even to praise his book to an admirer, for 'equally it is *your* book'.[3]

The work is meant to create its own readers by the process of their reading it; although (or perhaps because) alternative readings are open. 'It is hot music, a poem, a song, a comedy, a tragedy, a farce . . . it can even be regarded as a sort of machine; it works too.'[4] It is not susceptible, therefore, of analysis; the harmonies are to be heard, and played by ear, as they are written. 'One serious intention was to create a work of art – after a while it began to make a noise like music; when it made the wrong noise I altered it – when it seemed to make the right one, finally I kept it.'[5] The many and complex layers, the esoteric terms of its conception were to be reduced ultimately to simplicity; a simple melody in the improbable key of six sharps, such as Lowry once composed. Any 'explanation' is bound to be reductive. The basis is simple, the variations delicate. As D. H. Lawrence once said 'If you try to nail anything down in the novel, either it kills the novel, or the novel gets up and walks away with the nail.'

The twelve chapters cover twelve hours, from seven at morning to seven at night. Time both expands and contracts, although the pattern of the day is kept. The introductory chapter, which happens a year after the main events, dislocates time at the beginning, prevents any naïvely realistic approach; while it springs forward to the anniversary of the main events, it also reverts into the far past of the Consul's boyhood. We know 'the tick of real death, not the tick of time'.[6]

The jumble of recollection, prayer and delirium in the Consul's own mind in its zooming flights back and forth produce a syncopated rhythm not unlike that of the main structure. In his preface to the French edition, Lowry admits that his style may look as if he wanted to say six things at the same time instead of one after the other; yet the interweaving of past and present nowhere sets up unambiguous expectation. The mode which reveals the Consul's disintegration enables a thematic unity to evolve, but differently perhaps for each reader. The elements of this thematic unity are emblems – like, for instance the emblems of *Macbeth* – the Garden, the Pit, the Mountain, the Murdered Man, the Pariah Dog, the Horse.

Early in the day the Consul in his garden had 'seen' a dead man lying with a sombrero over his face, beside the swimming pool; but Lowry notes that precognition is a feature of 'really good D.T.s – Paracelsus will bear me out'.[7] In the central chapter on the *mirador*, the Consul takes a long look into the past and the future. Donne's *Hymn to God my God in my sickness* comes to his mind, turned into a golf song; then coming down from the *mirador*, he passes in the noon of the fiesta an Indian, gaily singing and riding a horse with 7 branded on his rump; the Indian whom he has just seen lying dead, whom he is to meet dying by the roadside some hours later.

The Ferris wheel, swinging like the cars that dangle from it, carries a multiplicity of interpretations; it is the wheel of Time, the wheel of the Law, the wheel of Buddha. When he climbs on this wheel to escape the beggar children, the Consul loses all his possessions, including possibly – it is not more than that – his vital passport, his identity. 'Nemesis, a pleasant ride' foreshadows the final spiralling downward of his body through the ravine, after he is shot.

As if circulating on a roundabout, minor figures reappear; the old woman with her dominoes whom he sees early in the morning, reappears in the last *cantina*. The pariah dogs, the vultures, the Indian's horse reappear too; although the Tarot pack is not directly invoked, the figure of the travelling Fool with a dog following him and attacking him, seems to represent the Consul (it is the Zero of the pack), as well as the Magician, the first card in trumps. At chapter VII, as Lowry said, the book begins to go into reverse, although even in chapter V, the scene in the garden, 'it is fast sinking into the action of the mind, away from normal action'. Hope appears for the last time in chapter IX, where in the most public and unsuitable of places, at the bull-throwing, the Consul seems able to express his love for his wife, to get in touch; but this is immediately followed by his destruction of all that has been won, when he insults her and runs away, towards the volcano and the sinister *cantina*, the Farolito, where he is shot by the local 'police'.

Lowry admits the construction does not allow of character drawing in the conventional sense, but 'there are a thousand writers who can draw adequate characters till all is blue for one who can tell you something new about hell-fire, and I am telling you something new about hell-fire'.[8]

The Consul of course hears voices, prompting him one way or the other way, that come from within, like the spirits of Dr Faustus. There is one image that evokes the sensation of a splitting mind and the loss of communication: 'The Consul had controlled his tongue. But he felt his mind divide and rise, like the two halves of a counterposed drawbridge, ticking, to permit passage of these noisome thoughts...' (p. 202). The memory of his wife's infidelity with his half-brother Hugh and his friend Laruelle, even though it sprang from her despair, is forced upon his mind by the presence of these two men, by the sight of Laruelle, obese and naked, in the shower. 'But the abominable impact upon his whole being ... that that hideously elongated cucuniform bundle of blue nerves and gills below the steaming unselfconscious stomach had sought its pleasure in his wife's body, brought him trembling to his feet' (p. 210).

At the beginning and the end of the tale come the love letters of the Consul to his wife and hers to him – unposted or unread cries of need and pain. They are divorced.

The Consul finally rejects the efforts of his wife and his

brother to save him as 'interference' and runs off – 'I choose hell ... because ... I like it.'

In front of the book Lowry set a passage from Bunyan's autobiography, *Grace Abounding to the Chief of Sinners:*

Now I blessed the condition of the dog and toad ...
they had no soul to perish under the everlasting weight
of Hell or Sin, as mine was like to do. Nay, and
though I saw this, felt this, and was broken in pieces
with it, yet that which added to my sorrow was, that
I could not find with all my soul that I did desire
deliverance.

The Consul's epitaph is spoken at the beginning by Dr Vigil: 'Sickness is not only in body but in that part used to be call: soul. Poor your friend, he spend his money on earth in such continuous tragedies.'

In his last moments the Consul identifies himself both with the dying Indian and with the thief whose blood-stained hands had clutched the stolen money. Although he tried to maintain a 'consular majesty' – even when found lying face down in the road by a Cambridge acquaintance, now a member of the Diplomatic Corps – the final word that comforts him is *'Compañero'* from an old fiddler, 'his face a mask of compassion'.

The Consul himself may have been guilty of war crimes in the World War, when he commanded a 'Q' ship named the *Samaritan*.[9] No one knows for certain. This infernal story, the far-off volcano of an earlier conflict, is reflected in the action of his younger brother Hugh, who is preparing to set out and sail an ammunition ship to the Spanish loyalists, running the blockade with a cargo of T.N.T.

The younger brother is 29 – Lowry's age when the events on which he draws occurred to himself.[10] Features of Lowry's own career are shared out between the two. As in Eliot's *Waste Land*, all the characters melt into each other; and, although some chapters are given from the point of view of Hugh, of Yvonne, or the film producer Laruelle, the Consul's view predominates, with its horrifying clarity, its moments of violence or hallucination, its fantasy. Nevertheless, the book is not just what he sees, nor is it pure horror or pathos.

The visions of a northern paradise, in Eridanus, are seen by Yvonne and Hugh, as well as the Consul; even in the last fatal *cantina*, the Farolito, as he lies in the arms of his succubus, Marie, he sees it depicted on a calendar behind the bed. The present, however, is Mexico, and Mexico, as Lowry explained, is a good place to set the struggle between powers of darkness and light. The Day of the Dead (All Souls' Day), a November fiesta half-way between Guy Fawkes and Hallowe'en, both gay and sinister, mixes mirth and death. The fiery brilliance of the Mexican temperament, the people's gallantry of mien and garb is given in Hugh's friend Juan Cerillo, and in Cervantes with his fighting cock. The macabre gaiety and more than Spanish brilliance of the land, in which every kind of landscape can be found, reinforces the courtesy, kindness, ferocity, cunning and cruelty of the people, their paradoxical mixture of qualities, Spanish and Indian. Life is lived in the *cantinas* and in the *plazas*, with their rich variety of names – but many suggesting the obscure wood where man is lost – *La Selva, El Bosque, Paris, Everybody Happy Including Me*, lastly the *Farolito* which opens at four o'clock in the morning, but from which the Consul can see the strange purity of the dawn and the oxen going out to work on the slopes of the mountain. This becomes for him a symbol of peace, somewhere beyond death; at the centre of the book, he had a vision of it. The worst characters have lively and often comic nicknames (such as A Few Fleas) and their broken speech can be both touching, as in the epitaph for the Consul – or comic-obscene, as in the menu offered to Yvonne: 'You like eggs, *senora*? Stepped on eggs. *Muy sabrosos.* Divorced eggs? . . . or you like poxy eggs, poxy on toast? Or spectral chicken of the house?' The day is crammed with events, improbably crammed in a realistic sense. Yvonne lands, bronzed and travelled, from her plane, the cosmopolitan American; Hugh, in his fantastic cowboy outfit, is about to depart. After a drink in the *cantina*, the Consul takes Yvonne home to breakfast, after which she rides with Hugh, her brother-in-law and former lover, through idyllic meadows: with the Consul they meet Laruelle, go to the fair, take the bus to see a bull-throwing, and go on to a restaurant for a swim and a meal. If this suggests Yvonne's desperate attempt to start up life again with her husband and to cover the embarrassment of meeting the other two men, it also allows for a good many comic interludes, including, in the early part the Consul as a comic drunkard. The Consul being shaved by his younger brother is like a figure in a *commedia dell'arte*; standing under the shower having turned on the taps in the basin, he waits for the cold water apprehensively. The Consul refusing all drinks and then rushing back to empty every one else's glasses (and the cocktail shaker as well) fits the macabre vitality of the Mexican scene itself, the bright colours and chocolate skulls, the craftsmen's stalls and the gaudy wood of the painted roundabouts, the sinister energy of the animals, and the watchfulness of the black-clad women. All four main characters, however, are exiles, cosmopolitan and rootless. The Consul is really an ex-Consul; his sad little office is closed.

The notices about sport, the cinema and the murals and sculptures leap to the eye of the passing journeyer; in

Laruelle's tower the Consul sees a strange mural of drunkards being cast into flames while the 'saved' float upwards, as Yvonne feels herself doing in the *Himmelfahrt* at the end. He prays: 'Christ, oh pharos[11] of the world, how and with what blind faith could one find one's way back . . . from a place where even love could not penetrate, and save in the thickest flames there was no courage? (p. 205). Edmund Wilson, speaking of Gogol, said his book was concerned with the forces in man which cause him to be terrified of himself. Lowry admitted the influence of Gogol, but he was also painting a picture of a particular time – the tragic thirties, when Spain was lost. The distant sounds of Europe beat through in Hugh's mind ('They are losing the battle of the Ebro!') but in the prologue–epilogue a grimmer war has started, for this is November 1939. The Consul's drunkenness is like the drunkenness of a world as it reels towards destruction. The Consul, who does not share Hugh's political activities (though his death is caused by the incriminating papers belonging to Hugh found in his pockets) will take no part in the conflict. He wants only to run away and live among the Indians, like William Blackstone, the Puritan. With all his formal associations with the British Raj (his childhood was spent in India) the Consul stumbles among the layers of Mexican civilisation, those radically different strata super-imposed on each other – a semi-Fascist group, the immediate past represented by Maximilian's palace, the older ruins whose very meaning is obscure, but whose gigantic forms dwarf the present state. The variety of Mexico makes it a microcosm; its beauty, an earthly paradise, but the paradise is full of snakes.

Under the Volcano is a triumph of craftsmanship; it was produced in ten years of writing and re-writing; if the texture is closely examined, there are phrases from

Lowry's earlier works at key points, and others which were to reappear subsequently.[12] Its continuity with the rest of his works should not obscure Lowry's habit of abandoning any achievement in which he had excelled, while retaining its imaginative life. *Under the Volcano* achieves its success by suppressing and selecting certain components. The cabbalistic and psychic aspects are not part of the overt design. The autobiographical basis was freely adapted from the facts of Lowry's stay in Mexico, his imprisonment at Oaxaca, his collapsing marriage. His wife left him in December 1937, he spent Christmas in jail; and finally his father's lawyers took charge of him and sent him to the USA in July 1938. The Mexican story is given a kind of run-through in Lowry's sequel *Dark as the Grave*, where the Consul is 'revived' in the person of an author revisiting the scene of his novel. The first and second Mexican visits are telescoped again in the sequel, *La Mordida*.

In *Dark as the Grave* 'Yvonne' (renamed Ruth) is described leaving her husband because he will not promise to stop drinking; the new discovery is that the original of 'Dr Vigil' who was also the original of 'Juan Cerillo' was murdered in a *cantina* when he was drunk. That is, the fate of the Consul has in fact overtaken his friend. Historically, Lowry made this discovery about *his* friend. The main concern of this work, however, is with the fate of the earlier book itself,[13] and the way in which history tends to repeat itself.

Another, and of course, fictional version of the events is given in Aiken's *Ushant*. 'D', the narrator, and the woman he is about to marry (Lorelei Three) are met at their arrival by 'Hambo', waving his stick, 'his trousers knotted round the waist with a necktie looking as if they might fall off at any minute and grinning at them shyly and affectionately and a little drunkenly'. He lives in a nest of rags on his verandah struggling with his book and his alcoholic misery, with 'the perpetual clack of the merciless high heels, the pitiless faithless heels along the tiled veranda and over and over into his heart' (p. 341). 'Nita' (Hambo's wife) had announced that she was going north to stay with her friends the two engineers at the silver mines; she was publicly declaring her intention of infidelity; all three sensing tragedy went to see her off at the bus, where 'the stonily beautiful little profile avoided the anguished and hang-dog gaze of poor Hambo, she was already looking ahead' to a gay and expensive holiday; the little gift of silver earrings which Hambo shyly and awkwardly handed through the window for her birthday was received almost with annoyance.[14]

Then, 'D' and Hambo reveal in talk that they had planned to share Nita, who had been 'D's' mistress, as one means of maintaining their curious relationship. This history must darken the relation of Laruelle and the Consul as much as Aiken's picture of 'Nita' darkens 'Yvonne'. Hambo attacks his friend:

> Yes, in the shadow of the Hundred Fountains at the
> Alhambra, you proposed to share her, as foul a sort
> of voyeur's incest as any second-rate god could
> imagine.
> True, admitted . . . but to hand her on to you, I
> could thus keep her . . . and twofold in function too, for
> this might stop you drinking . . .
> Very good. As we both saw instantly. I had her, the
> first night.
> Upstairs. And you looking over my shoulder.
> My chin was on it.
> I could hear you breathing.
> Yes, it worked.   (*Ushant*, p. 352)

'Nita' herself is not spared; 'D' says

Is such primal dirt really innocent? flawless and the
only really right thing? . . . The same brilliance, exactly,
the finest nuances of apparently ingenuous charm,
of gentleness, tenderness, and every note of it deceptive.
Her eyes flying like birds after every male . . .

(p. 355)

But she returns, and as 'D' and Lorelei Three drive away
the pair are left sitting either side of the fountain
'like Sacred and Profane Love'. It is doubtful which was
which. (Kilgallin gives Lowry a native mistress.)

Aiken thinks 'Hambo' had become a near-Communist,
and this aspect of the history is separately embodied in
Lowry's Hugh, together with memories of Lowry's first
voyage, his Cambridge days as a jazz player, and his rôle
of younger brother. Lowry himself hinted at some 'Sidney
Carton' act which got him into trouble in Mexico – it
could have been the loan of his passport.[15] He appeals to
his old friend in the same letter to look after his wife –
'For God's sake see she is all right. I foresaw my own fate
too deeply to involve her in it' (*Letters*, p. 13).

On Lowry's second visit of 1946, the great ravine was
found to have shrunk to a narrow gully. Indeed Conrad
Aiken describes a misadventure in which the drunken
Hambo fell into the open sewer which ran outside his
garden, and from which, covered in filth, he was hauled
out by his friend.

Characters prominent in the original story are not
included in *Under the Volcano*. The writing too was
shaped by the help of Lowry's second wife, to whom it
is dedicated. 'Though we're two and very different writers,
we're one organism, and in that regard I owe her a terrific
lot in the *Volcano*' wrote Lowry (*Letters*, p. 245). She
rescued the manuscript from the fire of 1944.

This novel most successfully joins the inner and the

outer worlds. The later works were sometimes modelled on it (the *Volcano* in reverse, as one was termed). The second phase of Lowry's work is by its nature less susceptible of treatment at novel-length being related to the dark forces of the mind for which alcohol is perhaps only a symbol ('Drinking is not the problem' as the hero of *Lunar Caustic* remarked). The psychic material struggled towards form, which was achieved in the Eridanus Quartet;[16] here, again, the inner and outer worlds could be joined. On the way there were struggles and failures, such as most novelists have experienced in the course of growth. It was on the basis of *Under the Volcano* that Lowry conceived his Dantesque trilogy, and although it remains imperfect, it may be claimed that the best of the later work deepens the effect of his greatest book, as it in turn clarifies what still, in these uncompleted works, remains embryonic and imperfectly mature. In other respects they go beyond it.

Here Lowry can be seen not only building his past life into the story, in metamorphosis, but also building his past books into the current one. His writing, in other words, is cumulative. Lowry, so proud of being at Cambridge the champion at bar bells, had set himself a weight-lifting of another kind.

Yet Mexico itself did not take root in his imagination in this way; the image remained clear, 'like far off mountains turned into clouds'. It was a land of sojourn; not, like England or Canada, to be dwelt in, but explored.

The book is built in a series of scenes, clear and detached. Very often the movement resembles that of a camera. As a child Lowry enjoyed films; his first and his second wife were film actresses. In the autumn of 1936 he and Jan went to Los Angeles, where he tried script writing with his friend Davenport. The technique of *Under the Volcano* frames certain scenes as if for the screen; it has been pointed out[17] how the long shots and close-ups of the approaching volcano, as seen through the window of the bus in chapter VIII), give a menacing impetus to the rush towards death. The mountain is seen sometimes near, sometimes distant; it is reflected in Yvonne's little mirror; the final rush through the forest towards the mountain makes it seem to lean forward over the valley.

Lowry's film world was of course that of the old silent screen; the early German films of the nineteen-twenties are recalled in the book itself, where there are everywhere advertisements for '*Las Manos de Orlac* con Peter Lorre'. The film tells of how a mad doctor grafted the hands of a murderer on to a mutilated musician; but *this* version is not the German original, it is a poor Hollywood copy. Similarly Yvonne's film career is told in the form of a cheap advertisement, recalled late in the story to give the flashback of her life before the final episode that parts her from the Consul. The use of advertisements both here and in later stories recalls the effect of film captions, interrupting the flow of the visual events with crude and simplified brevity.

The cinema's combination of intimacy with distance, no less than the way in which a film is built out of innumerable versions of each incident, taken, re-cut and reformed by the art of *montage*, powerfully suggests both Lowry's aim and the craft method which he employed in the composition of his works. He learnt from the cinema the art of suggestion, of collocation without comment, and transposed it into his own medium.

Two of the early stories indeed seem to contain between them the germ of *Under the Volcano*. 'A Rainy Night' depicts the inhuman indifference of a traveller to the plight of a dying man, though in this story the inhumanity arises from stupidity and not from secret fears. 'Satan in a Barrel' shows the Faustian end of the wicked

Judge Jeffreys – and when the Consul was first given a name he was called 'Jeff' or 'Jeffrey', the phonetic spelling of Geoffrey. The two stories, immature as they are, may serve to show how deeply rooted in Lowry's own art was this novel, as well as being rooted also in the works of other writers – Dante and Baudelaire, Marlowe and Shelley.

The first chapter throws a ceinture round the story – like the ceinture put round a ship in a later tale. It is thrown into the past; it ends with a double death, a finality that Lowry never used again. This in a sense, is an 'autopsy'. Even the early schoolboy stories had been given a frame, but the structure of the later tales is that of a past continuous with the present.

4

Strange Comfort Afforded by the Profession
(*Stories*, 1946–56)

In reality, every ego, so far from being a unity, is in the
highest degree a manifold world, a constellated heaven, a
chaos of forms, of states and stages, of inheritances and
potentialities.

(Hermann Hesse, *Steppenwolf*)

'You are possessed of Sigbjørn Wilderness; that is to say,
Sigbjørn is possessed by Wilderness. That is all right too,
although you have to make up your mind whom you
prefer.'

Dr Hippolyte, the Haitian Negro, whose background
includes Voodoo, is speaking as a scientist to the hero
of *Dark as the Grave*, the novelist Sigbjørn Wilderness.
This character appears in a number of later stories (once
as a diarist). Through this portrait of a novelist, Lowry
can treat the relation of the writer to his work and to the
raw material of life from which his work is built. The
character is discussed by Lowry himself in a letter to his
editor and friend in the spring of 1953, by which time
Dark as the Grave, on which Lowry had worked intermittently since 1946, was, together with its sequel, *La
Mordida*, entombed in a strong box at the bank from
which, in his lifetime it did not emerge.

Dark as the Grave is about the author of a novel like
Under the Volcano (but here called The Valley of the
Shadow of Death), reflecting in 'multiple schizophrenia' –
as Lowry termed it – the agonies of the psyche, with
drink as a sort of peripheral complication. 'Pirandello in
reverse, or Six Authors in Search of His Character; or
Every Man his own Laocoon' was to be a sort of 'Under
Under the Volcano'. It is a book about mourning; and

mourning produces splitting of the personality.[1] It seems that as a result of producing *Under the Volcano*, Lowry was driven to self-analysis of a destructive kind, perhaps because the book stood outside himself, another self.

The new story follows a journey made by the Lowrys to Mexico between November 1945 and March 1946. *Under the Volcano* had been written and despatched, and they were visiting the scene of the book, which Margerie Lowry had never known. When his publisher wrote suggesting a revision, Lowry composed the long apologia – having also, in a half-hearted attempt at suicide, slashed his wrists. His book was accepted before long; but the visit ended in a comic horrific series of accidents, culminating in the deportation of the Lowrys from Mexico as recorded in a sworn Statement (*Letters*, pp. 91–112). These form the basis of the sequel, *La Mordida*, set in Acapulco; in the course of the Statement Lowry says his friend Eddie Ford (Kent) and the British Vice Consul told him that trouble would have been avoided if he had given a small 'bite' or *mordida* to the first official that questioned him.

Dark as the Grave mourns the friend who was the original of Dr Vigil and Juan Cerillo, who, soon after Lowry left, had suffered the fate of the Consul. It mourns Nordahl Grieg, lost in a bomber over Berlin (during the flight to Mexico, which opens the book, Sigbjørn wonders 'How had Erikson felt when he knew they were going down?' (p. 33)); and it mourns too the burning of the novel of which Grieg was the co-hero, lost by the fire at Dollarton. Finally it mourns lost youth; Sigbjørn finds that 'By far the most potent ghost he had to encounter was himself' (p. 93).

The book is haunted by another Sigbjørn Wilderness, who has murdered his wife, and is being extradited from Mexico to Canada, whose story appears in the newspapers.² After his suicide bid, Wilderness I stands on the *mirador* (where in his novel the Consul had stood) and looking at the people below, he also sees another Wilderness there. 'But who was this other Wilderness standing beside them? A sense of fear of him, utterly ruthless was this other Wilderness. It was this Wilderness that had wanted the tower, not he' (p. 185).

In attempting to live through the events of eight years earlier, unknown forces are being released; after a period of abstinence, Sigbjørn has reverted to drink. He tells his wife soon after they land that 'it was my idea that my daimon was trying his hand at writing a book himself, rather than making me do it, since I've kept rather silent since the fire' (p. 86); some scenes from the past begin to repeat themselves like a 'disrupting film'. The landscape itself becomes unreal, he finds himself walking into a London cinema to see Poe's *Fall of the House of Usher*, and feels his whole life is being 'watched' – but who directed the film, himself, God, or the Devil? (p. 249). Sigbjørn is living the book he should be writing (p. 156).

The cost to Lowry himself was immense; he writes to his editor that it is 'worse than the Consul, and it is not an alcoholic hell. It is the abyss itself' (*Letters*, p. 291). Later he explains that he is seeking a new form, something like Chekhov's *Seagull*, or Pirandello; that the real protagonist of the book is man's unconscious. As for the 'persona' of Sigbjørn the writer, he is attacked rather violently as uninterested in literature, uncultured, unobservant, ignorant, but (and here comes the signal from Nordahl Grieg's work that we are in the realms of parapsychology) – 'What does he know? What he suspects is that he's not so much a writer as being written – this is where the terror comes in (It came in, just then)' (*Letters*, p. 332). An identity crisis had developed, and Lowry is being disrupted by his own creation, while writing

71

continues as a compulsive process that cannot be halted or controlled.[3]

Sigbjørn is at least not as violently attacked by his creator Lowry as the hero of the lost novel, *In Ballast to the White Sea*, who was 'a pathological liar – unable to give any rational account of himself, he invents the most fantastic tales about himself at every point that are so vivid they have a kind of life of their own' (*Letters*, p. 251). For even if his method is absurd, Sigbjørn thinks of his own book as 'a sort of mighty preposterous moral deed of some obscure sort, testifying to an underlying toughness of fibre or staying power in his character rather than to any particular aesthetic ability of the usual kind'.

Dark as the Grave is an obsessional work, without humour, though a happy ending is contrived: after discovering the murder of his friend, Sigbjørn drives back through a thriving countryside, whose improvement is due to the dead. The really obsessional feature, both within the book and in Lowry's comments, is that 'coincidences' or repetition of events seem of greater significance than the events themselves. The fact that the letter of rejection is brought by the little postman who is a character in the book that has been rejected; that in the sequel, the acceptance of the book should come to Sigbjørn as he stood on the *mirador* seems of more significance than the death of Martinez, his friend. The fact that Grieg was shot down in flames on the anniversary of the writer's wedding seems of more importance than the fact that he died. In this book, 'if the way forward is the way back', the ultimate mourning is for the writer himself, his 'lonely dying youth' (p. 252). Sigbjørn creeps out at dawn to the fatal last *cantina*, the Farolito of *Under the Volcano*, which is in the town where Lowry in fact was jailed. It is no longer there.

Dark is the Grave is not only about the writing of *Under the Volcano*, it is also about the effects of having written it. These were paradoxical and contradictory. On the one hand, having turned disaster into triumph, Lowry was exalted by the taste of success. He sent two cables to his family in England – one to his mother, one to his eldest brother – he boasted about getting into the *Encyclopaedia Britannica* ('For how long? Are you comfortable there, Malcolm?') and reacted intensely over adverse criticism, a piece of which is incorporated in the book.[4] On the other hand, he wrote verses

After publication of *Under the Volcano*

Success is like some horrible disaster,
Worse than your house burning, the sounds of ruination
As the roof tree falls following each other faster
While you stand, the helpless witness of your
     damnation.

Fame like a drunkard consumes the house of the soul
Exposing that you have worked for only this –
Ah, that I had never suffered this treacherous kiss
And had been left in darkness for ever to founder and
     fail.

(Selected Poems, p. 78)

He was no longer possessed by other writers, or by the need to write a great novel, since that ordeal had now been surmounted. The new ordeal was to struggle with the self, forgetting the advice of Dr Vigil 'Throw away your mind', to grapple with himself through his art.

The platitude that everyone always and inevitably talks about himself, since the contents of the mind are all that is directly accessible to the mind itself does not involve,

as Lowry well knew, embarking on 'the good ship Solipsism'. Yet he was more certain of the invasion of himself
by 'the daimon' than of anything else; whilst the attempt
to face further ordeal by direct handling of his own
drunkenness for words and its relation to the 'daimon'
set up a process of splitting. He could no longer follow
the way of 'Vigil Forget', who went ten miles in a
camión and a thousand on a freighter:

> no chameleon
> Changed colour faster than Vigil from apprehension
> Of himself. His cargo of disaster grew lighter and
> lighter.

till 'Feeling greater Than that ancient torturer, himself
... Ah! new selves' he finally turned round 'to board the
ferry to his whore' (*Selected Poems*, p. 20).

There are some new lights on the past story (Yvonne,
ironically renamed Ruth, becomes much less faithful and
sympathetic; a new character appears drawn from an old
enemy).[5] The second wife, Primrose Wilderness, is included rather than presented. A gay and relatively unconscious figure, she does not share her husband's
haunted world, but has come hoping to exorcise the past
as well as to enjoy the scenes of the novel. When Sigbjørn
says he is more afraid of Oaxaca than anywhere in the
world, she counters gaily 'Let's go to Oaxaca' – when he
adds 'Unless it's Cuernavaca' she responds 'Then let's go
to Cuernavaca as soon as we can' (pp. 81–2).

Any trust and security that underlies the nightmare
emanates from her:

> How beautiful and generous she was in her response
> to life. Ah, the times they had had before the fire. The
> quarrels after, when he was going to pieces, and he

74

had come near, perhaps, to driving her actually insane.
'Why don't you leave the man?' 'Because I love
him' . . . She was for him the spiritual life principle,
still allied to the earth, one of the elements too. And
again she was, as it were, herself a perceptiveness of
life . . . not a writer, but a person who loves life, who
express her creative life in the *living* of life. (p. 202)

But in subsequent stories, even 'Primrose' – or her succes-
sors – are distanced almost to invisibility.

The Divided Self, once the action is placed within, is
more readily treated in a short story than a novel. After
the autumn of 1952 Lowry seems to have tacitly abandoned *Dark as the Grave* and *La Mordida* – which together ran to a thousand pages – to concentrate on the
short stories collected in *Hear Us O Lord*, and finally on
October Ferry, which grew out of a short story designed
as part of that volume. The volume contains some of
Lowry's finest work and some of his weakest.

In 'Through the Panama' Wilderness now appears as
a diarist (he is also writing *La Mordida*). In other stories
he is described in the third person as a poet visiting Rome
on a Guggenheim Fellowship (Lowry applied for one
and even took his Cambridge M.A. for this end), as a
musician (briefly, in *October Ferry*), and as a drunkard.
The open and admitted disorder is greatest in the most
considerable of the tales, 'Through the Panama'; here the
hero of *La Mordida*, first named Martin Trumbaugh
(for Frankie Trumbauer, the saxophone player), breaks
from Sigbjørn and holds debates with him, attacking the
critics and also novelists. Here a character in a book
threatened to swamp and absorb the author.[6]

This diary follows another voyage of the Lowrys;
two years after the trip recorded in *Dark as the Grave*,

they sailed on 7 November 1947 from Vancouver in a
French liberty ship, the *s. s. Brest*, down the West Coast
and through the Panama, across the Atlantic to the port of
Le Havre, encountering a fierce storm off the Azores. This
journey starts on an ominous date for the Wildernesses (15
November)[7] and omens accumulate. One of the passengers is named Charon (this was apparently historically a
fact); the first ship they meet in the Atlantic is '*Flying
Enterprise*. A pretty name'[8] (notes Sigbjørn innocently).
But much happens before they reach that point. Off the
Mexican coast a nightmare begins for Sigbjørn, and
though he struggles to 'Turn this into triumph, the furies
into mercies' he feels his alienation may record a universal sense of dispossession, speaking through him (p. 31).
As the daimon is now on the job twenty-four hours a day,
a complete sense of death invades him, 'Man not en-
meshed but *killed* by his own book and the malign forces
it arouses. Wonderful theme. Buy planchette for necessary
dictation' (p. 38). He feels 'I am not I', but neither is he
one of his own characters; soon, however, paradoxically,
in a nightmare he enters some kind of trap, like a lock
in the canal where he 'is' the ship and also a voice and
also Martin Trumbaugh; Death appears as a jailer, with a
shattered face and shattered leg to lead him through the
gate of St Catharine's College Cambridge '*and the very
room*'.[9] Martin and Sigbjørn are now inextricably mixed,
though occasionally a general truth emerges – the real
cause of alcoholism is 'the ugliness and complete baffling
sterility of existence as *sold* to you'; yet Martin remembers overhearing someone say of himself 'The very sight
of that old bastard makes me happy for five days' (pp.
44–5). So their debate goes on; when it is over this period
is looked on as 'the bottom of all misery and wretchedness'
but after passing through the canal, the dialogue begins
again. A discussion of *La Mordida* and its author asserts

that neuroses and a kind of fierce health are stamped on everything he writes; that equilibrium, sobriety, moderation and wisdom 'those unpopular and unpleasant virtues, without which meditation and even goodness are impossible', must be turned into passions. More nightmares are followed by an attack on ignorance and even stupidity in the novelist, who is so fermentively creative that he can pay no attention to the ordinary world around him. This tortuous and contradictory passage includes an attack on realism ('Nothing indeed can be more unlike the actual experience of life than the average novelist's realistic portrayal of a character'). Martin feels himself quite apart from the rest of the human race; he cannot find his vision of life in any book; he does not think like other people, there is a painful conflict between him and reality; he even finds it hard to put on his clothes; and in general he is so tripped up by the complexities of his own nature that

Al stereles within a bote am I,
Amid the sea, betwexen windes two
That in contrarie standen evermo.

That this Ordeal is poetically conceived, at this point turning into a natural sea storm, does not prevent the tale being clogged with a good deal of psychological detritus. In the summer of 1952 Lowry was trying to get 'some of the nonsense out' (*Letters*, p. 335).

'Monsieur Lowry, he is the ancient mariner', the steward had said to Margerie Lowry (*Letters*, p. 159); in the diary the effect of the dialogue between Sigbjørn and Martin is reflected typographically: as Coleridge's poem has marginal notes, so long extracts from these appear beside the diurnal records; long passages from a dull *History* of the Panama Canal, lent to Sigbjørn by one of the officers, also appear. The passage through the Canal is an obvious symbol of rebirth and has been accorded the full Neo-Platonic treatment.[10] Sigbjørn himself annotates the significance of passing the watch towers, 'whence the control of the locks is operated', this is like writing a novel, with someone in another control tower above, watching the novelist's controls, and the different texts may offer a suggestion of Lowry's different and parallel 'versions' of his stories.

Parallel narrative and comment block the way for the reader, to make the meaning deliberately impenetrable, in the manner of certain modern French poets of the *Tel-Quel* group, such as Denis Roche. However, here and there, when Lowry gets back to the voyage, and his need for a drink, humour breaks in. He defends their liberty ship: 'It is wrong to suppose the poor old Liberty ship hasn't got a soul by this time, just because she was thrown together in 48 hours by washing-machine makers. What about me, thrown together by a cotton-broker in less than 5 minutes, 5 seconds perhaps?' (p. 72). On this voyage Lowry saw nothing of his own country; his stories that form the central group of *Hear Us O Lord* are set in Italy, which the Lowrys visited in 1948, before returning to Dollarton from France in January 1949. 'Strange Comfort afforded by the Profession' and 'Present State of Pompeii' are lucid; the much longer 'Elephant and Colosseum', though dear to Lowry, who ranked it with his best work, was (he realised) unlikely to appeal to others. He only begged his long-suffering agent not to tell him so. Its very grotesqueness may well mark a psychic break-through, the emergence of material that was afterwards to be reshaped for *October Ferry*. All these tales attempt a synthesis of past and present.

In 'Strange Comfort afforded by the Profession' a different Sigbjørn from earlier tales is in Rome visiting

Keats's House, with its relics of Keats and Shelley, and the Mamertine Prison, with its memories of ancient suffering ('the lower is the true prison'). He remembers how he visited Poe's House in Richmond, Virginia, and he feels ashamed to see all the relics of personal and intimate anguish, till he recovers from his notebook a letter he himself had written in such a moment – and which appears to be an actual letter of Lowry from the period of his greatest misery at Vancouver, when he was separated from Margerie. The 'Strange Comfort' lies in the identity and companionship of the dead, giving to the alienated a sense of belonging which modern writers, with their easy sound conformity ('more like folks than folks') cannot supply. The meeting of past and present here comforts the compulsive note-taker; Lowry has again begun to appropriate writers of the past, but in a new way. As one critic said, he pursues the topics read till they cease to be objects and become part of his own rendering of experience.[11] For historically he saw few old friends, and authors became a substitute for living company and for the lost family he was seeking, for his own dead youth.

'Present State of Pompeii', by contrast, offers a rational, critical, even humorous view of the threat imposed by the man-made ruins of today, the new volcanoes of pollution and destruction, surveyed by a Scots-Canadian schoolmaster, Roderick Fairhaven. Eridanus, his home, seen by moonlight with the Wildernesses in possession of it, hovers in his memory; beside him, vividly present, with a gaiety and tourist excitement like that of 'Primrose', is his wife Tansy, the Manx boatbuilder's daughter.

Roderick Fairhaven[12] can be alarmed if an archaic part of his mind intrudes into consciousness; he can be alarmed that his civilised mind takes a threat to the whole world less seriously than a threat to his own home. He thought

79

that 'the gods who wished to be believed should be wary of speaking too often through fire', remembering the horror of the fire at the oil refinery opposite Eridanus.

However, his actual horror of the ruins is enlivened by a guide, whose 'blasé obtuseness' parodies the simpler kind of literary explication; 'Bread and women, the first elements in life' he says proudly of the murals, '*Si*, first bread, then wine, then women . . . first elements of life, all symbolic!' But when asked if the volcano is now going to erupt, he first looks sombre, then again proud: 'Yesterday she give-a the beeg-a shake!'

'Elephant and Colosseum' registers a big psychic shake; as Dr Claggart would say in *Lunar Caustic*, it has some fine give-aways. Far from being as well settled in his home community as Fairhaven had been, Cosnahan finds his comic best-selling novel spurned in his native Isle of Man (in terms that recall Vancouver's reactions to Lowry). This novel treats of Lowry's early voyage, chronicled in *Ultramarine*, with the added news that Cosnahan, on that occasion, took part in a heroic rescue of a Japanese fishing boat, which was written up by his Manx quartermaster. On the home voyage, a cargo of animals destined for a zoo had been shipped, including an elephant. Cosnahan, who is greedy for praise and in search of a translator for his novel, can find no one he knows in Rome, till he goes to the zoo, where he meets and is greeted by Rosemary, his long-lost friend the elephant. Kennish Drumgold Cosnahan (who lives on Melville's New England coast, with his wife, an actress) is not only a Gaelic-speaking Manxman, but is possessed by supernatural powers (including water-divining) which he shares with his brother, both being sons of a Manx witch, Mother Drumgold, recently deceased, who modestly concealed her powers and died a Methodist.

On his return to his native isle, Cosnahan had been welcomed by a man who had been hanged but had survived this experience and was afterwards found innocent. Cosnahan perambulates, holding interior discourses with his 'other self', Drumgold, very amicably, although still feeling frustrated – since the publication of his book he has found himself unable to write. But when, after a preliminary warning of 'something' being imminent,[13] he meets Rosemary, he suddenly realises that his psychic powers and his power to write are one power, and that Rosemary the elephant who never forgets, 'so to say, was his work!' – his precious, ridiculous, second-rate work. He felt as happy as – why as happy as some old magician who has just brought off a master-stroke!

> Good God, he really was a magician! Or this was the real wild fount of his feeling shared, suddenly human . . . this that would have caused his book to have been translated, and by that, more than that, himself to be translated – his mother's son at last – into a conscious member of the human race. (p. 173)

Much here stems from Lowry's private myths. The mysterious Manx language which acts as a sort of *poésie concrète*, replacing Norwegian, continues the game of mystifying the reader; it links up with the Manx hymn 'Hear Us O Lord from Heaven Thy Dwelling Place' (which is a common Wesleyan hymn, that Lowry would certainly have heard at his Wesleyan school) and with an old boat-builder at Dollarton, a Manxman named Jimmy Craige who was one of Lowry's closest friends.

His own mother's death on her birthday, 6 December 1950, gave Lowry a share in her estate.[14] His mother's death must have affected him in unknown depths, but it also spurred him on to try to buy time from his publishers; to his chagrin, he found that this offer had been left so late that they had already decided to suspend the 'retainer' fees they were paying him.

The rather hysterical note of jesting and the humour, elephantine in every sense, of this tale, marks some kind of release. The younger son, Cosnahan, is a magician, a species of water-diviner.[15] His kind editor, Arthur, and the elder brother, whom he hopes to meet in Rome, certainly link Cosnahan with figures who have analogues in Lowry's own circle: his editor, Albert Erskine and Stuart Lowry did their best for him. He confessed in one of his letters that 'he once fell in love with an elephant' (*Letters*, p. 254), presumably on his first voyage.[16]

This tale represents that love of the bizarre that his brothers remember from Lowry's youth. It seems to represent for Lowry an act of recall and unification; his earliest novel, his mother's death, his own psychic powers, have somehow got between the pages of the same story. The agonised question of 'Through the Panama', 'Who am I?' has become a joke: 'Who was he? who was anybody? . . . man was Quayne, and man was Quaggan and man was Quillish, man was Qualtrough, man was Quirk and Quayle . . .' and several more, including the one who had been hanged.[17]

Lowry was not released from toil on his other works; he went on to struggle with the difficulty of trying to render the overlapping material consistent. 'The number of false starts and hen tracks on the page I have made had left me half dead with discouragement' he says in August 1952, nearly a year after 'Elephant and Colosseum'. But that curious work certainly marked an end to the ordeal that is recorded in the previous writings, for in sending this story to his agent Lowry said (of his plans for those works which he enumerates):

Some years back I was not equipped to tackle a plan

of this nature; now it seems to me, I've gone through
the necessary spiritual ordeals that have permitted me
to see the truth of what I'm getting at and to see the
whole business clearly; all that remains is to get myself into a material position where I can consummate
the ordeal by the further ordeal of writing it. (*Letters*,
p. 267)

After all, he had ventured to celebrate the strange comfort afforded by the profession, in Keats and Poe, whose
'sheer guts' and 'character, in a high sense of the word'
had enabled them, like shipmasters, to 'drive their leaky
commands full of valuable treasure at all costs, somehow, into port' among tempest and typhoons that rarely
abated (*Hear Us O Lord*, p. 108).

The different personae who succeed Wilderness, the
reasonable Fairhaven or the bizarre Cosnahan, represent
a different kind of splitting from the nightmare dialogue
of 'Through the Panama'. The drunken Wilderness in
'Gin and Goldenrod', the innocent, childlike, nameless
musician of 'The Forest Path to the Spring', Sturlesen of
'The Bravest Boat' (with a wife, Asta, who looks like his
sister) all live in Eridanus and are therefore specially protected. If each of these represents an aspect of the
author, it is an aspect defined and delineated for a
specific scene, and a specific tale; their characteristics are
not transparent disguises, but part of the 'Inner Society'
that makes up an integrated self.[18] Hence Lowry's in-
sistence that these tales should be read together, and that
only if read together do they give out the 'very beautiful
sound' he wanted (*Letters*, p. 335). In this respect they
serve as a tiny model of what he meant his great sequence
to become.

'The Bravest Boat' records a recited game of the two
married lovers on the shore at Stanley Park Vancouver,

as they go through the litany of a delightful fairy tale; the toy boat set adrift by the man, found years later by the girl, offers a playful ritual; it is based on a story read in the Vancouver papers, and shows the kind of co-incidence Lowry found everywhere. This idyll, with its companion at the close, frames the horrific central tales; and although the lynx in one, the cougar in the other, give a suggestion of terror, the beauty of the coast and the beauty of the relationship sound a very clear note of joy. The anguish, fantasy, realistic threats from society at large, and from weaknesses within unite to give a complete picture, or a harmonised chorus. In the succeeding book, *October Ferry*, which grew out of *Hear Us O Lord*, the different constituents, blended in that collection of tales, are united so that the work itself gains a much greater complexity, and is built upon counterposed stresses of paradox and contradiction.

October Ferry is in my view the sequel of *Under the Volcano*, in dealing with both an inner and outer theme of great power; both are centred on vital experiences in Lowry's own life.

The Strongest of Foundations: The Lightest of Structures
(*October Ferry to Gabriola*, 1947–57)

'It seems to be shaping up less like an ordinary book of tales than a sort of novel of an odd aeolian kind itself, i.e. it is more interrelated than it looks',[1] Lowry said of *Hear Us O Lord* (*Letters*, p. 320). He goes on 'The problem is really one of getting the greedy daimon in line and forcing him to do something lowly and unpretentious, even at the expense of working with logic and simple motives rather than with more glutinous danks and darks', although 'I don't share his memory' and 'having already written the book, as it were, he has no time problem'. The complex unity reflects in miniature the structure of the larger sequence of novels, planned on an ever vaster scale.

Three stories of Eridanus emerge complete;[2] the opening and closing idylls, which suggest a journey's ending, a Harbour View of life ('But ah! what storms they had come through!') 'The last of all brings the kind of majesty usually reserved for tragedy (God this sounds pompous) to bear on human integration and all that kind of thing; though it isn't my final word on the subject by a damn sight. I'm mighty proud of it' (*Letters*, p. 266). This pastoral, which might have as epigraph Wordsworth's 'Love had he found in huts where poor men lie' leaves the glutinous danks and darks to 'Gin and Goldenrod'; where Eridanus is being threatened both from without (by 'development') and from within (by shame and guilt,

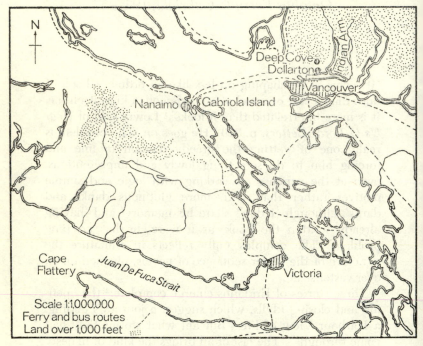

2. VANCOUVER BAY

and alcoholic outbreaks). It is naïve, but cunningly so.

Lowry's method of composition entailed constant writing and rewriting; several drafts were kept going simultaneously, like simultaneous games of chess (*Letters*, p. 344). The editor of *Dark as the Grave* described the three drafts as 'a formidable mess'. Lowry never looked on any text as final, not even in the case of *Under the Volcano*; the later works seem to have existed in a state of continuous recreation. Lowry explained at one time that every night he wrote five novels in his imagination, 'have total recall (whatever that means)' but was unable to write a word (*Letters*, p. 165). When in flow, he put everything in, on the principle that 'it was much better to get too much in than to get too little out' (*Dark as the Grave*, p. 155). The notebook method of composition, displayed in 'Through the Panama' also presented his editors with a formidable task of sifting his work and his transcriptions. Mrs Lowry's defence in depth of *Under the Volcano* applies even more strongly to the later works:

> I have lived five years with this book in its present form; it has been as much a part of our lives as eating and breathing. I am not blind to Malcolm's faults as a writer. His astonishing awareness of the thickness of life, of the layers, the depths, the abysses, interlocking and interrelated, causes him to write a symphony where anyone else would write a sonata or at most a concerto, and this makes his work sometimes appear dispersed, whereas actually the form and content have arisen so inextricably the one from the other that they cannot be dissociated. (*Letters*, p. 421)

The protagonist of 'The Forest Path to the Spring', a nameless musician, is writing an opera; this may suggest the correspondences and harmonies which evolved, but which are not meant to be explicit. The reader, however, is expected to work over his reading five times (*Letters*, p. 338), and to reduce the initial complexity to simplicity as Lowry himself had done – to make 'the machine' work for himself. This method, where the author shifted about 'like a xylophone player' reflected and sprang from Lowry's own shifts of mood, his mercurial temperament. Like the writer, he must feel the work shift and grow with his own life; the dynamic drive and rhythmic pulse of his own imagination should make it change, like the landscape of a rainy coast. Lowry's palette, with its 'glutinous danks and darks' may well recall the rich dark palette of Emily Carr, the greatest painter of British Columbia: her reseda greens, moss greens, mulberry, plum and pale-shining sunlight.

October Ferry, an ambitious piece of orchestration, combines the various moods of the tales in the earlier volume into a single story. The hero unites facets of the different selves that were separately presented before, as his moods – rational, political, ironic, or obsessive and anguished, fantastic and manic – succeed each other. In a first and most analytic look at himself Ethan Llewelyn sees that the 'sentient' life of its own which his cabin lives has induced in him feelings 'occasioned by tactile causes that have almost gone out of the world', so that something within himself was being demolished by the threat to his home (pp. 73–4).[3]

The sacred and living nature of the totem objects in a great empty forest land, expressed by the Indians in their carvings, enables Ethan to reject for himself the reductive term 'fixation', though Jacqueline, his wife, tells him his attachment to the place is 'really insane' (p. 199). He can hardly distinguish their love and life together from their cabin – a place which does not say 'I am yours' but 'You are mine'. Rebirth comes with a dive into the turquoise, life-giving tides of the inlet, and 'the first rationalities of love's survival' adhere in the very timbers themselves.

Lowry was proud of his own Canadian craft skills – his building, his swimming; and sometimes he would work at his manuscripts fifteen hours a day, at other times confesses to his long-suffering publisher that 'we have been a bit slack, a bit on the loafing side' although 'We rise at six and beam at the molten sun and swim much as of yore, only even better, save that we have lost our po' guitar in the sea; returned by Laocoon, when somewhat plastered, to Neptune' (*Letters*, p. 151). At other times a terrifying moment may release an inner storm, an abstract passion of hatred 'so all-consuming and so utterly implacable' that it feels like an invasion from 'the fearful wrath that was sweeping the world' or the Wendigo, the Indians' 'avenging, man-hating spirit of the wilderness' (*Hear Us O Lord*, p. 243).

To be possessed by a scene, by the inlet, or the spirit of the forest fire is to suffer an invasion by a power greater than the self; and this is hardly distinguishable from the action of the daimon, imperilling form in the work of art. In an earlier work, the artist's despair had been described by an image from the Rosicrucians (it is also found in Zen Buddhism), that of the Burning House.[4] As the universe is in continuous process of being created, so an organic work grows continuously in the creator's mind or perishes. The author is then like a man trying to rescue objects from a burning house: 'For is not the building, the work of art in question, long since perfect in the mind, and only rendered a vehicle of destruction by the effort to realize it, to transmute it upon paper?' The building burns while it is being salvaged; yet the work of art itself grows – 'even on paper something had happened to it'.

The power and truth of a concept, coming into being the moment it is postulated, works *against* the author, 'Not wishing to be postulated in such a fashion; for the truth does not stand still' (*Letters*, p. 291). The scheme for his novels which Lowry put forward varied from time to time; at one time *Under the Volcano* was the infernal component, till deeper infernos emerged; at one time the burnt work *In Ballast to the White Sea* represented paradise, at others *La Mordida* or the Eridanus 'Intermezzo'.[5] Form would not 'freeze' – Lowry could not tell if *October Ferry* would be 200 or 500 pages long, 'the plot of the novel gets into all the short stories'; some tales grow, while others, which he meant to expand, stay small. So in the end he would not release any of his material, but perpetually reshaped it.[6]

The best image of his style is provided by that other specimen of his craft, the light pier he built for his cabin, which, because it yielded to the tides, survived fierce gales.[7] The same elasticity is in his later writing. In the darkest novel, the pier becomes a symbol of achieved love:

> It was like their brave pier, most particularly and damnably like their very brave pier, which was not as might at first appear a barren symbol, for it was capable, if not of infinite, of continual extension, more over it was always having to be repaired, and while it had the strongest of foundations, it possessed also the lightest of structures and yet had borne the most violent tempests. Nor had it been built altogether by love; love never is. They had often cursed like stokers building it and quarrelled infamously.
>
> (*Dark as the Grave*, pp. 89–90)

In the letters it is continuously invoked as 'the most sentient object of my acquaintance . . . capable of crying and

singing and also of considerable anger, and I have also
fancied on occasion that it was talking to itself, doubtless
composing a subaqueous barnacly sort of poem' (*Letters*
p. 172).

Working in wood became a symbol for work in words;
it is a central theme in *October Ferry*, indeed the techni-
cal language of workers in wood seems to replace Norwegian and Manx as the inner private language of the
initiate. In response to an offer of a contract, Lowry
writes to his publisher about how his pier resists the
perils of tides, and of the heavy drifting logs (whose
menace beats on the mind of Ethan in chapter xiii of
October Ferry, 'The Tides of Eridanus'):

> We have not met anyone yet who has even bothered to
> think of a material explanation for its survival [Lowry
> wrote to his publisher], though there might be one,
> namely its simplicity, lightness, and freedom from top
> hamper; thus in a terrific sea – and it was overwhelmed,
> under water when we left – instead of giving way
> to the sea and lifting from its foundations, it simply
> and calmly clung to the beach and stayed where it
> was, the foundation being just slightly heavier than
> the overall plankings . . . wood *floats*, and will try and
> float even if nailed down, and if overwhelmed by
> water, the heavier it is, the harder it will pull at the
> nails – and all round guess there is some sort of lesson –
> apart from an image – in this, the more so since the
> foundations in this case, simply and contrariwise
> adjusted themselves to the undermining of the beach,
> instead of vice versa, and became securer than ever.
>
> (*Letters*, p. 305)

Writing from his last exile in England – for such it was,
Dollarton was home – Lowry pleaded that the pier is to

be cherished even if it isn't there; and the final destruction of what 'was in a sense *us*, we risked our lives building it' shattered him. 'Nobody could understand how it survived so long, not even engineers, and it was nicknamed "The Crazy Wonder" on the beach . . . Margie and I built it together with practically no tools and I am broken hearted it is gone' (*Letters*, p. 388). The structure of Lowry's latest works is very light and the interconnections are not at all evident. On the other hand, the foundations are very strong, in the sense that each book cumulates and absorbs the previous books, and its many layers include images that go back to childhood. The combination of fragility and rooted strength arises from the method of writing and the free, almost random mixing of overlapping versions; this allows craftsmanship to combine with spontaneity. William Empson began a poem

> Magnolias for instance, when in bud,
> Are right in doing anything they can think of . . .
> Their texture can impose their architecture.

This is how Lowry's style works; his texture can impose his architecture. In his later tale, the feelings blended are as complex as the whole range of stories; the whole scale, from the realistic to the fantastic, can be found in *October Ferry*. The naïvety persists, the cunning increases and the idyll includes its terrors.

Historically, the Lowrys took the ride by bus and ferry in search of a new home on Gabriola Island in October 1946; their original joint story, rewritten by Lowry, had by January 1953 become a novel. It cost him more to write than *Under the Volcano*. In July 1955 – he was then in England – Lowry's doctor forbade him to handle this theme, yet in the last few months of his life he seems to have tried again. It was edited by Mrs Lowry.

As in *Under the Volcano*, a public theme is united to a story whose roots are within the hero. Pollution and destruction of natural beauty advances till something like the Mexican fresco of Rivera is invoked – 'the only thing lacking is a picture of Progress in the form of Jesus Christ driving a locomotive through a virgin forest'.[8] At this time, the dangers of despoiling the environment were not generally acknowledged and such countermeasures as a Department of the Environment unthought of. Eviction of the whole community of Dollarton squatters was in any case sought in the name of Progress by the municipality. After Lowry's death, the whole settlement was demolished to make a park.

The inner theme of *October Ferry* is that of a haunted man, devoured by remorse and the recurrent memory of a friend's suicide at college, which the hero cannot forget. since he incited it by his own despairing mockery, coupled with a promise to 'follow'. His Furies materialise in the form of an advertisement, featuring his dead friend's portrait, which pursues him across Canada as part of the horrible advance of Progress: it works rather like a jerky film. A series of other advertisements, like the captions of an old silent movie, add their preposterous commands and questions and savage jokes to the haunting. The bus journey, a flight, an eviction itself, is very extended; while the earlier flight across Canada, three thousand miles by train, takes one page to record. If fear of eviction and guilt of murder, the 'murder in the heart' are eventually transformed into mercies, yet the bus journey in parts grows horrific – Lowry indeed termed this novel 'Satanic' and was progressively terrified of the feelings he aroused in himself by writing it. The stages of the bus allow an even greater immediacy than the diary form of 'Through the Panama'. If Ethan Llewelyn's sin, like his namesake in Hawthorne's story, was to carry a marble heart in his

93

breast,[9] he is cursed also with psychic powers. It is a sailors' superstition that the drowning experience a total recall; something like this happens on the bus journey. There are three flashbacks, two being accompanied by the memory of films. The memory of Llewelyn's courtship in Toronto in 1938 is associated with the film *Outward Bound*. The posthumous voyage in that film seems reflected in later events. The Llewelyns find the Gabriola Ferry, a nameless boat, painted a sinister yellow.[10] The second film, *Isn't Life Wonderful?*, a tale of ordeals and eviction, had been seen by the Llewelyns just before their betrothal, and offers a true prophecy of their future struggles.

The second main flashback is concerned with the destruction by fire in 1946 of Ethan's ancestral home at Niagara-on-the-Lake, and with this a comic-horrific series of outbreaks of fire, seemingly the work of poltergeists rather than pyromaniacs; this is associated with the film of *The Wandering Jew*, and a further series of coincidences, all of a terrifying, Satanic kind.[11] Another film, *Wuthering Heights*, stresses the dark haunted aspect of Ethan's life his 'Heathcliff' aspect. When life is most unreal it resembles a film. This note is sounded three times (pp. 49, 287, 299). In a city apartment even love only feels like a film about love. 'It was as if they had exchanged sunlight on water for photographs of sunlight on water', the sounds of spring for the kind of incidental music that goes with documentaries.

The last flashback – the scene of the suicide's room in Ixion's College, University of Ely – is evoked by the advertisement, a kind of jerky moving cartoon of pictures about Mother Gettle's Kettle-simmered Soup. The hysterical and magical aspects of this novel become comic when Jacqueline Llewelyn is given a magician for a parent, whose acts far outdo those of Mother Drumgold in 'Elephant and Colosseum'. He bears some resemblance to McGregor Mathers, founder of the Order of the Golden Dawn. He is a chief of Clan, of royal descent, Jacqueline is his illegitimate child by an emancipated female of equally noble Scots descent who committed suicide and left her baby on its father's doorstep. All this, told at the beginning, effectually explodes any realistic approach to this novel – though Ethan early denounces all novels which 'possessed secretly no reality for him at all' (p. 61) – 'nothing was more unreal than a novel, even a realistic novel' (p. 184).[12]

He is not an artist of any kind, but a criminal lawyer turned carpenter, although he sometimes composes rhymes which are apt to be made up of lines from other poets. And he has never been an alcoholic.[13]

The story retains traces of the fantasies surrounding Cosnahan, yet there is an aspect of Llewelyn which is more like the rational schoolmaster Fairhaven. He has a sardonic wit, heard when he reverts to the accent of the English public school (as at the Rugby match, 'Drop a goal, there, why don't you?'). During his engagement, Ethan had told Jacqueline of childhood miseries which give an enlarged picture of those of Lowry himself; she counters with her much more horrific story. In the nightmare period after the fire that burnt their home in 1946, misinterpreting his wife's anguish, Ethan blames himself for it and works out a devastating case against himself from her point of view. This case is directed against a figure not unlike Aiken's Hambo. One of the criticisms he, as Counsel for the Prosecution, imagines his wife putting against him is 'Was not the most dishonest and plausible thing he had ever done to pretend to lay all the blame for this at the door of his own childhood?' (pp. 108–9). He indicts himself as a man dedicated to Ordeals, who expects his wife to follow his labyrinth of expiation; a man who under a mask of likeableness, good looks, humour, an air of success and everyday sense of adventure, had cheated by offering her something that was no life for a woman; a man who perhaps really was accursed.

Ethan can be protective, responsible, a man of the world. His wife, like himself, is sensitive to psychic intimations which they call being 'in the current'; a recurrent image to express the effect of psychic shock is that of death by lightning.[14] Yet the cabbalistic talk of Jacqueline's father is mocked as 'holy gibberish', the language of the occult is rejected for being high-flown; Ethan prefers the language of boatbuilders, since for him Eridanus has been his cabbala 'a means less of accumulating than of divesting oneself of unbalanced ideas, by balancing them against their opposites' which is 'a process not unlike that of psychoanalysis' (p. 169). As the end of the journey approaches, even Ixion's fiery wheel is imaginatively transformed by the talk of an old Manx carpenter and coachbuilder (p. 231). Ixion's wheel is of course St Catharine's wheel, the arms of Lowry's own college at Cambridge.

Ethan is capable of such crisp language as 'come now, less evil omens, my love. She's no more an evil omen than you are!' Jacqueline is seen vividly and distinctly, compared with the earlier Primrose or Tansy; she is allowed tantrums, disappointments, even a tendency to seek refuge in drink; the two quarrel, if only briefly, for the inner weather quickly clears. Jacqueline in tears 'like a little tree divesting itself of rain, shook from herself a merry cascade of laughter' (p. 271); alight with an idea, she dances naked out of bed 'Excited as a little cookstove, when the kindling catches in the morning, and you have to close the damper' (p. 201), or furious, she cries 'What you don't see is that I'm only too glad to get away from your goddam shack!' (p. 191). There is a level on which

96

the book *is* realistic; the relation between the two is seen more dramatically than before. Jacqueline's grief after the fire, which Ethan misinterprets, is due to the knowledge that she can never have another child; part of his transformation is that he suddenly sees the demands of her life as different from his own, sees her need for security conflicting with her devotion; his conscience begins to work more rationally.

After the fire, Ethan's anguish had reached a pitch of desolation that was beyond avail in a region where 'thoughts broke up, precepts long abandoned stumbled on';[15] but this depth evoked a sense of its opposite, a feeling that somewhere must be a triumphant counterpart to this disillumination (pp. 146–7); in time the whole thing faded to something like a waking dream endured under morphine.

Both Llewelyns endure together a tempest of the mind, which blows like the great wind of the Indians, the Chinook, bringing them a sense of sorrows not their own, till Ethan wonders if Nature herself is having some sort of breakdown. At another time, he sees the burning of his home as some holocaustic revenge the war had taken on him, remembering some of the burnt ruins of Europe, especially the church at St Malo. Church bells are one of the recurrent themes of this novel; but the echoes and resonances need not be registered consciously. They will be felt like 'the engines of those huge invisible tankers at night hugging the opposite bank that telephoned through the water to them in bed an aberrant commotion like submarine motorbikes' (p. 75).

The darkest moment comes at a block at a level-crossing, where the clanking of the train and the clicking of windscreen wipers, with the remains of a hangover, precipitate Llewelyn into the depths; the face of the dead boy confronts him one more:

97

> And at this moment, as abruptly as the machinery of a
> phonograph with self-changing records clashes into
> action, it was as though within him a totally different
> consciousness had taken over . . . this other conscious-
> ness familiar and feared, had been rising swiftly to the
> surface of his mind and had now taken command.
>
> (p. 209)

The Counsel for the Prosecution is arraigning him: Llewelyn, though skilled to defend murderers without, is
powerless to defend the murderer within. Lowry justified
his work as a 'thematic collision of material and im-
material, shadow and substance, unreality and reality',
adding emphatically 'If he [the author] can't make his
novel move horizontally, he certainly feels that here he
proves he can do it vertically' (*Letters*, p. 362).

The presiding literary genius is that of Edgar Allan Poe,
whose anniversary coincides with the anniversary of the
friend's death, which is also the day of the bus ride. But
the novel draws on the full American tradition, down to
Faulkner, whose combination of disordered minds and
deep local influences offers a parallel to Lowry.

Omens are plentiful but ordeals are surmounted. The
fire that burnt their home had already been transformed
at Eridanus into a gay and lovely firework display (celebrated with their small son, a self-absorbed child who
lives in the wings throughout the drama).[16] Somehow this
last experience at the level-crossing dissolves Ethan's ob-
session, and the next time he sees the dreaded advertisement it has turned into something vaguely ludicrous in-
volving 'the war effort' which (at the level of collective
good works) only arouses his scorn.[17]

The bus journey ends in a town that is like a toy, with
an absurd row of fortune tellers' haunts to parody the
cabbalistic wisdom of Jacqueline's father, a ship that

looks like a toy liner in the harbour, a tiny bastion of the Hudson's Bay Company's trading days that now houses an estate office. In the person of the waiter who serves in a pub (one half of which is old and beautiful, and one half modern and hideous) Ethan meets a man he had once defended in a murder case, which even in memory remains something of a joke. It is still with almost Kafka-like difficulty that the ferry is found, and it needs two starts, but at last they are off, having arrived at the auspicious hour of noon and waited until five.

Quite early in the story, the Llewelyns had entertained in a light way the idea of leaving Eridanus: 'That impermanence, indeed, the ramshackle tenuity of the life, were part of its beauty. The scene too that confronted them through their casement windows was ever-changing; the mountains, the sea, never looked the same two minutes on end; then why be afraid of change?' (p. 171). Yet now to leave it is to undergo a kind of death; the ferry is in a sense Charon's boat. A glimpse of his home across the gulf awakens new thoughts in Ethan of throwing himself overboard. He meets in 'this chapel perilous' an old priest from the island who gives him consolation; he is then uplifted once more and feels in tune with his destiny. Heaven at once supplies a Rabelaisian answer.

> Ouch!
> 'Hail to the seagull in the empyrean!
> Who man's head useth, as a spare latrine!' (p. 307)

Echoes of the earlier half of the book begin to come through like the fulfilment of magic riddles in a fairy tale. At the time of the fire Ethan had found himself in jail for stopping to help some motorists and had protested he was 'no sozzled Samaritan'. Now as the ferry turns back to land a sick passenger (and a drunk who had come aboard by mistake) he succours the afflicted lady with a swig of gin.[18] The parody of *Under the Volcano* is plain enough; it is *Under the Volcano* 'in reverse'.

As the boat speeds back to Nanaimo, Ethan experiences the sense of a mysterious order. There is nothing like a series of misfortunes to make hard-won battles against the irrational collapse and to invoke a primitive mode of thought; but this mode is no longer Satanic. It is neutralised, if not benevolent. The psychic world suddenly loses its terror:

> Like light but quicker than light, this spirit must be,
> and able to be in a thousand places at once in a
> thousand disguises, most of them, as befits our
> intelligence, absurd, this spirit that terrifies without
> terror, but that endeavours, above all to communicate,
> to say no more than perhaps, 'Hold on, I am here!'
> p. 320).

The secret language of psychic intimation is only to remind us that we are 'not unwatched'.

Immediately Ethan experiences a feeling that something very important is about to happen; as the ferry regains the harbour, it picks up the evening papers, where now amid preposterous news and advertisements, the Llewelyns read:

ERIDANUS SQUATTERS REPRIEVED

If 'Canada's beauty was in its wildness, and if you like untidiness. It was the only originality it has', Llewelyn could feel at times, against his better judgement and some of the evidence, 'some final wisdom would arise out of Canada that would save not only Canada herself, but the world' (pp. 133, 202).

But their decision to leave Eridanus has been taken;

the decision to renounce it is in some mysterious way a decision of hard-won exorcism. At dusk they reach the island, where the fires are beneficent, lit by the settlers to clear their land; while a shower of meteors attests the benevolence of heaven. On the way out the second time from the harbour, the ferry passed a little toy boat – the Bravest Boat itself, perhaps – bobbing in the open sea.

The pattern caught up from other works is thickly woven here. There are a number of echoes of themes from *Under the Volcano*.[19] The correspondences with the stories of *Hear Us O Lord* are naturally closest, and range from casual references to the Wildernesses and Fairhavens as neighbours, to the visible presence of the Manx carpenter, who actually gets on the bus. A number of benevolent but unintelligible old men, would-be guides and helpers, crop up, just as, in the earlier part of the journey, the bus passes several burning houses and other sinister sights and stories. These correspondences could have been discovered by a reader of the whole sequence, but the reshaping of material from the lost novel, *In Ballast to the White Sea*, is a 'deep laid anchor' which would not be recognisable except for Lowry's account of the early work in his *Letters*.[20] The double start to the voyage, the two brothers, of whom the elder is a lawyer and the younger a sailor, are merely narrative conventions. Here in *October Ferry* Lowry kills off the younger brother on this voyage; his name, Gwyn, means White, and the White Sea is said by Lowry to have been a symbol of death. In the lost novel by Lowry, the hero incited a 'Dostoievskian brother' to commit suicide;[21] here such recurrent versions of the one theme are symbolised finally in the bar-tender's pyramid of glasses – 'a creative process, an act of magic' reflecting and multiplying the scene outside – 'the reflected windows flowing upward . . . a multiplicity of lighthouses, seabirds, suns, fishing crafts, passenger boats, Australia-bound colliers' (p. 250) – a reflected multiplicity of worlds. This image is the best definition of Lowry's own art.

The fires that gleam with portentous and supernatural frequency through this work are akin to the fire of the stokehold in the earlier work. That awed phrase attributed once to Nordahl Grieg 'What do we know?' is, however, here ruthlessly parodied and reduced, at three crucial points in the story, to the colloquial 'Well, what do you know?'[22] But 'the life of the imagination and life itself has been saved', as before.

Lowry has almost succeeded in reproducing between his own works the kinds of correspondences he regarded as ominous in daily living; he himself is playing the superior intelligence to his own characters and even to his readers.

October Ferry is rooted in his own actual life at Dollarton and in his deepest concerns, the fear of eviction, and of encroachment, the need to find another home; the story of a boy murderer, Chester or Chapman (who is also mentioned in other stories of Eridanus) was the reflection of a historic case about which Lowry felt deeply.[23] To have drawn such intractable and frightening material into a form controlled, balanced and even witty and detached, demands that the artist extend himself. Here and there the application of a phrase from Bishop Berkeley – 'the reality of heaven as physical pleasure' – or a medieval definition of God 'whose centre is everywhere and circumference nowhere', is lightly and confidently made; but at the same time the scene is realised with exact precision. The seagulls who had deflated Llewelyn's idea of harmony are seen 'steadily and faithfully *rowing* back to Nanaimo with them' to where 'the flag still *galloped* aloft at the Post Office'. The sure thrust and long steady glide of the birds' wings is caught in the verb with a reflected grace. Lowry drew seagulls in his letters as a sign of happiness.

The humour of the book, its contradictions, and its ability to 'resolve the immedicable horror of opposites' can best be seen as the summing of much work that has gone before. Its detachment had not been approached since *Under the Volcano*. Lowry himself regarded the writing of this tale as a matter of sanity, if not of life and death for him, and the achievement as 'a psychological triumph of the first order'. He felt that it would survive if only because 'the bloody agony of the writer is so patently extreme that it creates a kind of power in itself!' Although 'symbols are pointed at blatantly instead of being concealed or subsumed in the material, or better still, simply not there at all . . . It's all done on purpose' (*Letters*, pp. 338–9).

Floating submerged in this narrative are images from Lowry's early days; his childhood in its dark but also in its rosier aspects, in the more poetic and indirect forms suggested in the opening chapter. Perhaps indeed the carefree little boy, rather indifferent to his parents, and devoted to his schoolmates, the ten-year-old son of Ethan and Jacqueline, serves as reincarnation of something that had been lost from the author's life. For his declared aim in this novel was to show how the protagonist could be brought by a shock to the reinterpretation of his own past.

Schoolboys appear as guardians to an unhappy smaller boy in one unpublished short story from Dollarton.

'Enter One in Sumptuous Armour' depicts with Dutch fidelity a home on Deeside, a ride across to Lime Street Station, the journey from Liverpool to a public school in Cambridge, and the course of a spring term in which Dick and his friend Harold Stoker, like good Scouts, help a miserable newcomer, victim of 'ragging', to transform his power of kicking against the pricks until he becomes the heroic goalkeeper of the house hockey team. They themselves fail to win the places they covet.

Dick shuttles back and forth from an unsociable home – he enjoys a good game of golf, but has never entered a pub, and gets to the cinema only infrequently – to the narrowness of school life where 'I was very unpopular, less on my own account than because of my brother's vast reputation'. However, as sub-prefect, he metes out corporal punishment to the juniors who are ragging the new boy, Raoul Snow, in whose figure all the misery is concentrated. Dick loves his parents – 'It was difficult to explain the fear I had of discrediting them, of hurting them': Raoul is motherless, and his father has a sinister club-foot.

This competent five-section narrative could well have been submitted to any Canadian provincial newspaper, like the sketches of his housemaster which Lowry once published. 'Mr Chips' here appears under his real nickname 'The Balf'. However, scrawled in the margin are demonic notes in Lowry's tiny script, putting in the horrors. Cooke the gardener is rechristened Ghostkeeper, blindness and crippling emerge, there are notes for an unwritten section where Raoul tries to hang himself with his pyjama cord. The title itself contains a grim private joke; its 'armour', ostensibly the goalkeeper's padding, in the original context (Shakespeare's *Troilus and Cressida*, v, 6, 26) suggests early death. It recalls too that derisive Valentine which the Leys *Fortnightly* gave to Lowry at the height of his scathing hockey reporting 'Do, rudeness; do, Camel, do, do' (*Troilus and Cressida*, ii, 1, 31, Thersites to Ajax).

Names are symbolic, and link up with Lowry's private mythology. When Dick's parents praise him as 'a fine boy' he mysteriously replies 'Dick was a fine whale too', with

104

an obvious reference to Moby Dick. The tormenting of new boys is termed 'nip-on'; the pun on Japan, marginally noted, suggests Lowry's own painful initiation in the Yokohama brothel.

As Dick and the newcomer Snow both represent different aspects of Lowry, there is a sinister resonance in the elder brother's teasing: ' "What are you going to do with him? Throw him overboard?" He said this so disarmingly, it could not be considered cruel. "Maybe he'll push you overboard." ' (p. 10). Finally, at the height of his triumph, the two responsible and fatherly young sub-prefects ask Snow if he likes this job? He answers 'Yes – and no.'

As the alternative version to the miseries of 'An Autopsy' – it incorporates some material from the poem on the dead gardener quoted above, p. 36 – this story, in its minute fidelity to a landscape and a scene implies a pathos more convincing than the marginal terrors which crawl round the typescript, trying to worm their way in. It is written by one of Lowry's many 'selves' – the rare one who enjoys a balanced view without being anything of an artist. Transformation has not really occurred, except in the cryptic parting advice of the two family servants to Dick. From the chauffeur, an old soldier, the voice of Richard Grenville of the *Revenge* – 'Chew glass and spit blood'; from the gardener, the wisdom of Reynard the Fox – 'Run away laughing'. These two aspects of Lowry may be met in his biography; he drank and he bolted.

The story witnesses to Lowry's uncanny power of recall, since its origins can be traced to the last shot fired in the duel between 'Camel', the sarcastic hockey reporter, and his schoolmates. Just before he left for his Far Eastern voyage, Lowry was reported in *The Fortnightly* as playing for a house team in the position coveted in the story by Dick and Harold:

March 1927   Lowry on the wing was hardworking and gave the necessary humorous touch to the game. One of his kicks in particular was worthy of any goalkeeper – but it was unfortunately in the wrong direction.

6

Charon's ferry

... un, che al passo
Passava Stige colle piante asciutte.
(Inferno, ix, 80–1)

In renouncing that paradisal home 'that I loved or love
more than my life', Lowry followed the path of exile as
supreme ordeal, sustained as always by his art; 'I think
of nothing else but poetry when I'm not thinking of my
old shack on Burrard Inlet' *(Letters,* pp. 408, 410, 414).
By returning to an earlier bereavement, reliving and re-
covering strength from it, the 'splitting' that follows
mourning became healed; in the interior country of the
heart, the boundaries of hell moved backward, and from
what long had been a silent area in Lowry's memories, a
searing flash from adolescence blazed. In 'Through the
Panama', Death himself showed Sigbjørn Wilderness the
gates of hell as the great portal of St Catharine's College
Cambridge;[1] in *October Ferry,* the historic event is recalled. It remains still relevant only as a means to establish the conventions of Lowry's art so that these can be
identified.

Charon's Ferry and the Gates of Dis are ancient symbols of the narrow way, the pangs of constriction and the
reversal of constriction. Lowry associated *October Ferry*
with Dante's *Inferno* and did not feel himself to be the
author of this 'Satanic' work.[2] The doctrine of Ordeal,
explicitly recognised from his own early days,[3] developed
from the crude transformation of childhood into a series
of physical ordeals, to the recognition that the spiritual
ordeals of living are but a preparation for the final ordeal
of writing *(Letters,* p. 267).

107

Lowry's primal landscape is that through which in the fourteenth century passed Sir Gawain in his quest for the Green Knight. Chivalrous knightly romance presents ordeals of initiation and purgation – a form of trial. In religious terms, suffering transformed into enlightenment becomes available for others. Lowry felt early the desire to 'use hardships', and also to assume the rôles of father, of mother, to 'postulate the responsibility for both' (*Ultramarine*, p. 102). He cast the rôle of his protagonist in the likeness of Christus Patiens ('An Autopsy'), Faust (*Under the Volcano*), various heroes of Poe and Melville, Cain. In his maturest work, he reflects 'I wonder whether it is not man's ordeal to make his contrition active.' In converting evil objects of his past to present use, he makes one hero prefigure something he should have done to his own past, which must be turned into use for others (*Hear Us O Lord*, pp. 180, 179).

To any child who lives on the Mersey, the ferry gives the first taste of ships; it is also the first step to exile from Maternal Eden, the approach to unknown worlds, father's way to work.

A sinister ferry opens Lowry's first published tale, 'Goya the Obscure', where the hero crosses to his haunted Liverpool of sexual sickness, and fear.

> Imprisoned in a Liverpool of self,
> I haunt the gutted arcades of the past.[4]

In *Under the Volcano*, a sinister little rhyme incorporating a children's chant plays itself in the mind of the Consul as he sets off with his brother:

> Plingen, plangen, aufgefangen
> Swingen, swangen, at my side,

Pootle, footle, off to Bootle
Nemesis, a pleasant ride.[5]

In later tales, ship's engines sing a nursery song, *Frère Jacques*, and in that most haunted tale, 'Through the Panama', even the noises of the ship's ventilators sing, aeolian expressions of mood, akin to dreams.

An unpublished verse, entitled *Freighter, 1940*, recounts a launching at Birkenhead during the blitz, ominously amending the traditional signal[6] to 'God may not bless thee, dear, but may sustain', as the ship moves into a Dantesque world – under an ambiguous rainy heaven, on a dangerous tide, with a subaqueous peopled darkness below.

The ferry, quiet as Charon's boat, knows death.[7]
A gangway, medieval, spans the moat.
Pier Head, and the bells prance out. We are careful,
Looking up. Gulls, bombs, manna, all may fall,
Below the sea, in the tunnel, men breathe . . .

As the ship recedes, dwindles, moves out to the bar in bitter weather, the ominous scene of Lowry's first tale, *Goya the Obscure*, is revived. The scenes of his childhood followed Lowry, as Wordsworth felt himself pursued by the shadow of a peak beyond his lake, that

Towered up between me and the stars, and still,
For so it seemed, with purpose of its own
And measured motion, like a living thing,
Strode after me.

'Outward Bound . . . but are we going to heaven or hell? But they are the same place you see' (*October Ferry*, pp. 13, 252).

Lowry's historic ordeals began at prep. school. A letter from a schoolmate in the Leys file makes them explicit. At ten or eleven Malcolm, 'somewhat fat and clumsy, with a very uncertain temper', was victimised by one of the masters, who, 'a bit of a sadist, seemed to take a particular delight in singling out Lowry and another boy (not a Leysian) for the application of his riding switch, with what seemed very little pretext'. Lowry was ragged by other boys for the humiliating reason that he had the habit of breaking wind in his sleep on such a loud and prolonged scale that it woke up the dormitory which expressed its feeling 'forcibly'.

As Ethan Llewelyn remembered at the Rugby match 'the bloody obscene cruelty of those fiendish little beasts of children when they had someone like me at their mercy' his hands trembled, though he was cool enough about the floggings administered by a junior master (*October Ferry*, p. 21). He remembered how it hurt to be beaten on his chilblains – and these, not blindness or lameness, were Lowry's genuine but ignoble affliction as a child.[8]

Between his fourteenth and seventeenth years, at the Leys School in Cambridge, Lowry made transition from the world of sport to that of writing and pop music, encouraged by his housemaster, W. H. Balgarnie (the original Mr Chips), and by a young English master. One of his prizes was *The Hairy Ape*. The impressions of the boys and masters vary widely, recording the different impact of those stresses and splittings that come with adolescence.[9] One recalls the arrival of 'a small boy, tousle-headed, splay-footed, ruddy faced, all teeth and perpetually grinning – frightfully jaunty and argumentative, rather untidy, terribly fond of talking and especially fond of listening to sea yarns which I was rather too prone to tell in class, and he would often trap me into

110

telling them'; another the youth 'tough physically and
mentally, a little blasé and casual in manner, something
of a lone wolf, and with a questing mind mature beyond
his years. He had a sense of humour and his armoury
against foolishness included a rather cynical little smile
which would flicker momentarily on his lips. It was very
eloquent.'[10] And when playing jazz with Ronnie Hill, he
would mark the rhythmic breaks with triumphant farts
(Day, p. 88).

The new found power of words is celebrated in the
second half of the 'Autopsy' on his childhood (which
opened with self-pity and identification with Christ's
passion):

> Matriculated into life by this, remembering how
> This laggard self was last in the school Marathon,
> Or that he was last, last in everything,
> Devoid of all save wandering attention –
> Wandering is the word defines our man –
> But turned to discover Clare in the poor snail[11]
> And weave a fearful vision of his own.

The youngest of a family is commonly plagued with
anxiety from the need to run fast to keep up with the
others.[12] Physically stronger than his next brother but
unable to fit in with team games, Malcolm faced his
ordeal of adolescence and its conflicts, armed with a
cynical humour, and power to evoke the fantastic and
macabre; to the cries of protest against the sarcasm of his
sports notices in *The Fortnightly* he replied: 'One of you
remarks that I have undoubted talent; this is an error of
etiquette – you should never tell people that they have
undoubted talent; you will find me making no such mistake with you.' At the Rugger match, Ethan indulges in
accents of easy patronage that recall this early triumph of

111

brain over brawn. The same accent re-occurs whenever 'the schoolmasters of literature' are attacked; nothing was more infuriating than to be told 'You are not nearly so unusual as you think you are!' (*Ultramarine*, p. 96).

The short stories and verses written at school turn anguish into jokes, as in 'The Light that Failed Not', echoing in its title Kipling's tragic tale, or 'Der Tag', recording a painful blunder;[13] others are concerned with hypnotism and hauntings, melancholy grave-yards complete with corpulent toads; but in one or two, failure in compassion and inner conviction of Satanic guilt are crudely but powerfully adumbrated.

Some verses from Chaucer prefixed to *Ultramarine* sum up the taste for ordeals that drove Lowry from his parents' ideal of comfort and provision:

> Take any brid and put it in a cage
> And do al thyn entente and thy corage
> To fostre it tenderly with mete and drinke
> Of alle deyntees that thou canst bithinke
> And keep it al-so clenly as thou may
> And be his cage of gold never so gay
> Yet hath this brid by twenty thousand fold
> Levere in a forest that is rude and cold
> Gon ete wormes and swich wrecchedness.

One shipmate, an acquaintance of Wilfrid, who records that the story of Hilliot's failure to rescue the captive bird from being eaten by a shark and his excessive remorse is historically true,[14] records too the more humiliating ordeal, concealed in *Ultramarine* under the story of Olga, when Lowry was mocked for sexual inadequacy by a Japanese girl, a mockery that the sailor echoes.[15] Yet he adds 'What a man he was', includes a verse of a jaunty jazz song, *Marching down the road to China*, and observes that Lowry wanted very much to shine, but seemed like a lost soul.

The drunken sequence in *Ultramarine* is the heart of the book; it is both a celebration of release, and a violent explosion of the mind into fragmented experience, made up of wanderings, reading, fear, remorse and dreams of grandeur.

None of Lowry's later romantic accretions to this voyage appears in the seaman's record; but it constituted Lowry's sole experience as a wage-earner, his sole experience of living under orders. His return after two years to Cambridge, to a college a few yards from his school, sometimes felt 'a horrible regression', which was used very briefly as part of Hugh Firmin's story in *Under the Volcano* and at more length in the lost novel *In Ballast to the White Sea*.[16] Imaginatively it was rebuilt only in *October Ferry*, in the story of the suicide of Peter Cordwainer.

A Londoner of nineteen, Paul Launcelot Charles Fitte, son of a company director, went up from Harrow School to St Catharine's College in the same term as Lowry, Michaelmas 1929. On 15 November 1929, the *Cambridge Daily News* carried a story under the headline 'CAM-BRIDGE TRAGEDY. STUDENT FOUND DEAD IN GAS-FILLED ROOM'. Next day the inquest was fully reported, and after Fitte's father, the chief witness was described as 'Clement Milton Lowry, an undergraduate at St Catharine's College Cambridge' the last person to see Fitte alive, who

said he first made acquaintance with the deceased in Germany, where they were studying languages. The last time he saw him was the night of Thursday, 14th. He seemed slightly upset. He was in bed, and seemed

rather pale and depressed. He told witness he had had
a smash with a car, and in consequence was feeling ill
and upset. Witness supposed he was upset about that.
Deceased seemed curiously reserved.

Deceased told witness something about the circumstances of the smash. While witness was there, deceased
received a telegram 'Please send money tomorrow without fail' and read it out to witness. He made a remark
more sardonically than humorously. He explained to
witness that he owed some money and that was why
the telegram was sent. He seemed worried . . . Reply-
ing to the Coroner, witness said deceased did mention
suicide to him, but only jokingly – not seriously. 'I think
he was so level headed' added witness 'that it was the
last thing in the world he would do'.

The irony of this observation appears to have been un-
observed or unintended.

Towards the end of the time witness was with him,
deceased cheered up . . . He laughed sardonically and
said 'I must get out of this'.
Coroner: Get out of what – out of this world? – He
said it after he got the telegram, but only humorously.

The expected verdict of 'temporary insanity', the words
of consolation to the father, and the coroner's comments
that the telegram (signed 'Phonia') was 'rather peculiar'
reveal nothing.[17]

The pitiful story is substantially, but not in detail, that
of Peter Cordwainer, as told in *October Ferry*. In order
to coincide with the death of Edgar Allan Poe, this had
to happen in October, but in 'Through the Panama'
Fitte's actual date of death, 15 November, is recorded
with a peculiar horror, there unexplained. After Ethan

had left Peter's rooms 'at Ixion in the University of Ely' (p. 47 – later described as the University of South Wales), his friends in the pub had shouted 'Let the bugger die!'

> Remorse, yes, he still felt shattering remorse, but was it remorse that made him want to talk about it, embroidering the whole damn mess with senseless inventions, or rather that he felt in some sense proud of the appalling thing he had not prevented from coming to pass? (p. 50)

The story hinted at and gradually unfolded, culminates in chapter xxvii, 'Useful Knots and How to Tie them', but an earlier recollected conversation injects the sting of authenticity by the same mixture of the macabre and the jaunty that Lowry had developed at school

> 'All right, Mr Peter Bloody Cordwainer . . . Go ahead and do it. Grandmother won't let you down, I'm sure . . . She's got a lot of friends in high office. And besides the Tibetans say you can be comfortable even in hell, just so long as you're clever. As you are, if not so damn clever as you used to be. I've promised you, I'll get in touch with you through old Goddo's wife on Sunday afternoons!' Had he said this? Or Peter 'It's almost worth doing it just to see the expression on all those stick-in-the-mud faces at Ixion tomorrow.' 'You forget you won't be here to see them, old man.' 'That's right, nor will I. That's funny. But I thought you said . . .' 'Not for three days, I think, as a rule . . . Anyway, you're going to do it sooner or later, so why not now? Have another spot of gin, old chap.' 'Thanks, old man . . . Ethan, you come too!' 'No. You do it. We'll keep in touch. I'll come later. The same way.' 'Then before you go, I . . .

115

wouldn't you–?' 'None of that'. 'And don't fail me!'
(pp. 68–9)

The Russian roulette may not have been quite like this;
but neither the effect of a few careless words nor the
weight of remorse can be estimated in human, biographical terms. Although Fitte had been seen by a doctor, who
came while Lowry was present and prescribed a mild
sedative, Lowry was the last to see him before Fitte
stuffed up the crevices and turned on the gas jet.

In *October Ferry*, Peter Cordwainer is not Fitte but a
ghost built from memories of Fitte and other memories
recalling also an unfortunate member of the Pentacle
Club, the amateur conjurors' club at Cambridge, who
strangled himself after he had tied himself up in knots
as an experiment.[18] Cordwainer hangs himself. He had
been a bully at Ethan's school, but also a close friend;
a success, a good Scout; he is recalled to Ethan by
the chirpy boastings of a small boy on the bus, chronicling
his vacation journeys. Through his association with advertisements (in one he appears with a chain of brothers,
following Mother Gettle) he is linked with the menace
of the present, the so-called March of Progress that
threatens Eridanus; by sharing the anniversary with
Edgar Allan Poe, he evokes the 'haunted man' in Ethan.
He is akin to the *Doppelgänger*, the 'second Wilderness', who appears in *Dark as the Grave*; he has an
element of the author's 'lonely lost youth' within him,
as seen from middle age.

Lowry concealed the story of Paul Fitte from his
parents, though he may have told Aiken, who some
months later described Lowry to himself as 'a small boy
pursued by furies' (*Letters*, p. 8).[19] Two of his schoolboy
stories from *The Fortnightly* seem to anticipate the
trauma; in the more realistic, a starving Swedish fireman

tells his pitiful tale to an uncomprehending stranger; in the other, a play is enacted in a dream, where the wicked Judge Jeffreys of the Bloody Assize is sent a halter by an enemy and ends in despair and damnation, haunted by 'voices' of his good and evil angels; it has already been suggested that they anticipate *Under the Volcano* (see p. 67 above).

Such psychic anticipations had already been observed by Lowry as part of the greatest ordeal of his youth. The effects of drink, the struggles at writing, were compounded by shock into a fear of psychic sensitivity. This found its form in the identification with Nordahl Grieg, the feeling of being 'drawn to the fire of the stokehold', to further ordeals. The contradiction of his fighting and incompatible selves became even more disruptive. The *psi* factor in his own experience seems to have become potent, adding to shock an increase in psychic turbulence.

The memory of senior dons bears out that Lowry was frequently run in by the police for being drunk. (He was also turned out of his college lodgings.) Yet he continued his brother Stuart's tough sport of weight-lifting with bar bells and his own success at jazz. Although becoming extremely shy, shunning company, he made one or two deep friendships which persisted for life – with Martin Case, Gerald Noxon and John Davenport particularly. In June 1931, having taken the first part of his Tripos, he appealed to Aiken, confessing 'a despairing and rather disordered existence'; he felt within 'the need to identify a finer scene', but feared that Aiken would term this only a form of escape, 'wanting alternatively to kill Liverpool and myself'. In *October Ferry*, Ethan remembers that after Cordwainer's death he 'stood apart, self-condemned, a kind of pariah, and imperceptibly his colleagues had tended to feel that too...'; he 'tended to see people in groups, excluding him' (pp. 41–3).

Yet at Cambridge Lowry remained superbly confident in his own powers as a writer, and the one thing everybody knew about him was that he was going to write a great novel. He did succeed in finishing *Ultramarine*. In the later, lost novel, set largely in Cambridge, the hero confided his torments to 'a Dostoievskian brother' who instead of being sympathetic 'is scornful of the whole business and accuses him of every abominable tendency under the sun and several not under it'. (During a visit to Haiti in 1946-7, Lowry saw a Voodoo ceremony – which is the nearest he ever came to magic rites – and the ordeal of walking through the flames; this was used as a dream sequence in the unfinished *La Mordida*.)

In *October Ferry* Lowry returns openly to a writer who influenced members of his circle at Cambridge – among them Gerald Noxon and Humphrey Jennings. Charles Fort's *Lo!* (1931), a bizarre cosmology, records extraordinary natural phenomena, especially showers of objects from the sky (teleportation), typhoons, earthquakes, poltergeists. Arbitrary battering by unrelated marvels witnesses to an underlying unity; the cosmic theory ultimately evolved is Ptolemaic. In *October Ferry*, Fort is invoked to support the comic-horrific sequence, 'The Element follows you around, Sir', treating of the burning of the house, which as Lowry later told a Cambridge friend, was the worst event of his life; though at the end of the book these cosmic threats are transformed to a benign shower of meteors, greeting the arrival of the travellers at their haven. Showers of meteors were a speciality of Fort. A taste for the bizarre that had long been seen in Lowry was erected by Fort into a principle, and the discovery of this book had been 'a red letter day in my life' (*Letters*, p. 26) because it 'made the inexplicable dramatic'.

Lo! opens abruptly:

A naked man in a City street – the track of horses in
volcanic mud – the mystery of a reindeer's ears – a
huge black form, like a whale in the sky and it drips
red drops as if attacked by celestial swordfish – an
appalling cherub appears in the sea –
Confusions
Showers of frogs and blizzards of snails – gushes of
periwinkles down from the sky –
But the underlying oneness in all confusions. (pp. 7–8)[20]

Lowry early discovered Kafka and Hermann Hesse; he
read Dante for his Tripos. These works gave him images.
Soon appeared Dante's Hellgate, across the dark ferry, the
Maison Dieu of the Tarot pack, the Burning House of
Zen Buddhism, the Black Tower of Yeats. In *Lunar
Caustic*, it is the gate of the hospital closing upon the in-
mates with a sound like shipwreck. In *Under the Volcano*,
Laruelle's tower bears within a terrifying mural of the
pains of the damned; from the *mirador* above, the Consul
looks out over the *barranca* to a heavenly scene beyond
death, but then he plummets, and his choice is decisive.
The same tower dominates the early part of *Dark as the
Grave* and is the scene of the attempted suicide. In
'Through the Panama', the towers of the canal locks become emblems of a higher control over man; in *October
Ferry* the gates of the level-crossing set the scene where a
secondary personality rises to overwhelm the hitherto
dominant representative of reason and conscience; before
Ethan rises the face of Peter Cordwainer 'handsome,
grinning'. Later, the heavenly gate is represented by the
tiny bastion of the Hudson's Bay Company which guards
the entry to the Ferry, and to release.

From *Lunar Caustic* of twenty years earlier, associated
figures of youth and age, the Young Murderer and the
Wandering Jew, reappear in this novel, while the magic

119

Mother of 'Elephant and Colosseum' is replaced by an even more powerful Magic Parent of the male sex, the drunken McCandless, a man who has accepted his own guilt.

The spring of life, the fountain, is first dreamed of in that scene where the representative of government, the Consul, lying face downward in the gutter, is roused by an English voice, a 'King's Parade' voice, and sees a Samaritan with a tie 'mnemonic of a fountain in a great court' bending over him. 'The Consul brushed the dust from his clothes; he sought for wounds in vain; there was not a scratch. He saw the fountain distinctly. *Might a soul bathe there and be clean? (Under the Volcano,* p. 84). The striped tie calls up the fountain in Trinity Great Court (Gerald Noxon's College), calls up also Andrew Marvell, scholar of Trinity, and his pastoral world:

Clorinda	Near this, a Fountaines liquid Bell
	Tinkles within a hollow shell.
Damon	Might a soul bathe there and be clean,
	Or slake its Drought?

Clorinda and Damon, lines 113–16[21]

Lowry's astonishing power of recall, testified to by his friends, included many dream memories; yet observing the physical flash of lovely movement could evoke its equivalent from a far buried past.[22] Among the horrors encountered along the Bell–Proteus path in 'The Forest Path to the Spring' was not only the beautiful, fierce mountain beast, but the discarded halter flung across the path. Salvaged memories, rising unbidden, were built into these works, 'the soul computes when much of its domain is lost'. The reward, 'prize of long kinship with disaster' is 'the power to readjust the dead'[23] and to project a state far more disintegrated than the ordinary alcoholic's.

And shall I tell them, every one
Of the good of the soul scrubbed to the bone ...

Out of such images of terror was compounded the layered and laminated prose, with its annealed and bonded fusions, its 'provisions made for every reader' (*Letters*, p. 66). From this 'desolate sense of alienation, possibly universal sense of dispossession', the writer works, using himself as a rabbit for vivisection (*Hear Us O Lord*, p. 31). Even the gusts of fear, guilt or anger can be controlled, mocked; or impulses to murder or suicide can be reflected in art. So, the Gorgon's head, reflected in the shield of Perseus, becomes transformed from menace into armour. The ordeals of an unstable temperament become the substance of works whose richness lies in their many-faceted reflections; for this, however, a fixed determination of purpose must underlie the instability.

The price of insight is suffering; to uncover what an instinct of self-preservation has repressed taking on a burden greater than it is possible to recognise fully with the conscious mind. As in accepting the role of Cain Lowry assumed a guilt greater than his own, he gained the power to go on. His failure in compassion had been, when disclosed, a small sin – but perhaps the Consul's imputed war crime shows its *effect* on Lowry.

A friend of Cambridge days writes:

I think Malcolm does emerge as the man *qui tollit peccata mundi*, who had assumed the rôle of Cain which becomes at last the redemptive rôle through his own descent into hell, his own acceptance of the sins of the world ... he has taken on the rôle of the guilty in order to atone for all kinds of private and social sins, in a way that in *October Ferry* does break the bounds between himself and all other people on the ferry, bound for Paradise.

Alteration of mood and personality led to the writer's responsibility. An underlying steadiness, that almost Puritan sense of duty in his family, is reborn in him on the far side of despair.[24] Instead of banning drink like his father, by rejecting the pursuit of order and duty, he banned that limited sense of obligation which is open to the man who conforms. His father was a self-made man; Malcolm Lowry painfully unmade and divested himself, till in this act of decreation he crossed by Charon's ferry into those strange visionary countries 'not in Mexico but in the heart'. At the end of *La Mordida*, he quits this country:

> What had died was himself, and what came about
> through these confusions, these oscillations, these
> misunderstandings and lies and disasters, these
> weavings to and fro, these treacheries, these
> projections of the past upon the present, of the
> imagination upon reality, that out of these dislocations
> of time, these configurations of unreality, and the
> collapse of will, out of these all but incommunicable
> agonies, as of the mind and heart stretched and
> attenuated beyond endurance on an eternal rack, out
> of arrant cowardice before little danger, and bravery
> in the face of what seemed slight to overcome, and
> heartbreak, and longing, had been born, darkly and
> tremulously, a soul. (p. 445)

The Cambridge of Malcolm Lowry

Although Lowry was only three months younger than myself, he came up to Cambridge two years later, into a university where English sparkled, the liveliest of the Arts faculties. His own college, St Catharine's, was very strong in the subject, but Tom Henn who directed studies there seems to have been found unsympathetic by Lowry. Conrad Knickerbocker writes with extreme hostility of Henn; and yet in 'The Ordeal of Sigbjørn Wilderness', one of Lowry's unpublished stories from the latest period of his life, the manuscript opens with a letter to Tom Henn (who has always maintained a gentlemanly reticence about Lowry). Tom Henn was perhaps too obviously the kind of father-figure Lowry wanted to escape. A man whose ancestors were judges and soldiers, who had lived adventurously in his boyhood in County Clare, carrying a gun (unloaded) on patrol round the grounds of his home during the bad times of the Irish Civil War, Tom Henn was not likely to be impressed by Lowry's adventures – and as his perceptive shipmate has recorded 'he wanted very much to shine'.

The only memory of Lowry at St Catharine's preserved by his contemporary, Professor A. R. Humphreys, is of his going to read a paper to the Shirley Society on the hardships of a seaman's life, in a state of advanced intoxication. But the literary circles of Cambridge knew Lowry well (he was copied by a small admiring group, who aped his walk) and he could not but share in the intellectual

123

excitement of the writers' set that included Empson, then writing *Seven Types of Ambiguity* (1930), Jacob Bronowski, helping to edit the magazine *Experiment*, Kathleen Raine, Alistair Cooke, T. H. White, Julian Trevelyan, and Humphrey Jennings, the brilliant young film producer. These formed a loose literary group, interested in Surrealism, Eliot, Joyce, Lawrence, Salvador Dali, Paul Klee. They kept up a flow of publications, ran exhibitions and even some private printing presses. *Experiment* and *The Venture* were published from 1929–32. Malcolm Lowry's friend John Davenport published in *Cambridge Poetry* (Hogarth Press, 1929) some lines which suggest the chief figures from the past who acted as guardians

> Eliot, Rabelais, Dryden, Donne
> Bless the bed that I lie on,
> Blake and Rimbaud, Marvell, Voltaire,
> Swift, Joyce, Proust and Baudelaire.

but the heaviest influence, here and elsewhere in that volume, is that of *The Waste Land.*

The literary influence of Lowry's more formal English studies can be seen chiefly in what must have constituted his work for the Tragedy paper in Part II of the Tripos. Naturally, he looked hard at Ibsen and especially *Ghosts.* The Hidden God of one of his latest stories is named Henrik Ghostkeeper, while the row of little tombstones that Hilliot of *Ultramarine* discovers in Norway (his uncles and aunts, infants 'all knocked for a row of milk bottles') suggests a gloomy history of syphilis in a dark northern fjord. Lowry may have got a special interest in Scandinavia from a fellow of Queens', L. J. Potts; the translation of Nordahl Grieg's novel, *The Ship Sails On,* which so captivated him, was by none other than the Master of his own college, Dr Chaytor.

A sinister echo from the chorus of the Furies in Aeschylus' *Eumenides* sounds in *Ultramarine*; reading of Shakespeare and Marlowe, begun at school, shaped the powerful blend of despair and comedy in *Under the Volcano*. The total determinism of Ibsen's *Ghosts* or Cocteau's *Infernal Machine* is invoked in the sinister coincidences and dark forces of later works. The passage of the Panama Canal, in whose locks ships mount and sink (controlled from on high by men in watchtowers, who in turn are controlled from higher still) suggests iron tyrannies, while the heavenly and infernal voices of 'Ghostkeeper' are at least more ambiguous. Yet a free spirit also blows through these later works, a *pneuma*, a wind whose echoes may be as lovely as those of Coleridge's Aeolian Harp.

> O the one life within us and abroad,
> Which meets all motion and becomes its soul,
> A light in sound, a sound like power in light,
> Rhythm in all things, and joyance everywhere . . .
> And what if all of animated Nature
> Be but organic harps diversely framed,
> That tremble into thought, as o'er them sweeps
> Plastic and vast, one intellectual breeze,
> At once the soul of each and God of all?

(*The Ancient Mariner* was perhaps not the only Coleridge poem Lowry read.) Interpenetration of the natural and the invisible worlds in the world of common life – the Spirit of the Deeps taking a bus ride – as it is found in Lowry's own writing reflects the inclusive forms of Tragedy, and the interweaving of the familiar and the uncanny that this genre initiates.

In the nineteen-twenties, English studies at Cambridge

were unique in England in laying stress on contemporary and comparative literature. Although he was driven to consult a crystal-gazer about the form of his examination questions on Dante, Lowry's reading of French and Italian left its mark. He was not an academic, but he was bookish, and much of his reading stuck for the rest of his life. The young lecturer who had done most to reshape the Tripos, I. A. Richards, was both stimulating and yet given to doom-laden prophecy. In his autobiographical novel, *Lions and Shadows, an Education in the Twenties* (Hogarth Press, 1938), Christopher Isherwood, who read history at Corpus 1923–5, describes the excitement of hearing Richards proclaim 'in his plaintive baa-lamb voice: "According to me, it is quite possible that in fifty years' time, people will have stopped writing poetry altogether".'[1] His mixture of boyish games and boyish desperation ends when Isherwood contrives to get himself sent down by deliberately failing his Tripos (first ceremoniously dropping Stubbs' *Charters* into the Cam). He had kept up a spirited struggle with the 'poshocracy' – the ruling clique of smart undergraduates – but having gone down he bought a small Browning automatic pistol; made a will; in his Journal raved against himself, though from time to time cheerfulness broke in:

> No. No. No. It was hopeless. As long as I remained at home, I could never expect to escape from my familiar, tiresome, despicable self. Very well, then, I would leave home. I would start all over again, among new people who didn't know me. I would never see any of my old friends again – well, at any rate, not for ten years. I would go to Mexico, to Paris, to a mining village in Wales. (p. 197)

Isherwood describes the sense in his generation of being

overshadowed by the First World War, the great 'Test of manhood' in which they had *not* been initiated; this made them feel inferior. So he next decided to write a novel, to be named *The North-West Passage*, in which he descibed the plight of his neurotic hero, the Truly Weak Man.

> 'The truly strong man', calm, balanced, aware of his strength, sits drinking quietly in the bar; it is not necessary for him to try to prove to himself he is not afraid, by joining the Foreign Legion, seeking out the most dangerous wild animals in the remotest tropical jungles, leaving his comfortable home in a snowstorm to climb the impossible glacier. In other words, the Test exists only for the Truly Weak Man; no matter whether he passes it or whether he fails, he cannot alter his essential nature. (p. 207)

So the Truly Weak Man takes the terrible north-west passage, avoiding life; and his end, if he does not turn back, is to be lost for ever in the blizzard and the ice, a sort of voluntary sacrifice, a slow suicide.

Christopher Isherwood did not make the acquaintance of Malcolm Lowry till many years later; but the moods depicted in *Lions and Shadows* are near to Lowry's moods.

At this time, the political implications of the rise of Fascism were not clear, and political dangers did not begin to make an impact till about 1933 with the rise of Hitler, when Lowry had already left Cambridge. However, Lowry became directly involved with the most advanced political household in the Cambridge of his day – that of J.B.S. and Charlotte Haldane.[2] Her third novel, *I Bring Not Peace* (Chatto, 1932), has been briefly mentioned in the Prologue. Not only does the central figure bear a recognisable likeness, though distorted, to Lowry, but the story ends with the suicide of Fitte (here called Cowling), carrying rather explicit traces of black-mail and homosexuality. The main scene of the tale is Paris; its defiance of convention is based on a smart flippancy.

Not surprisingly, the portrait of the young American jazz player, James Dowd, did not please Lowry. He is associated with the Rimbaud of the *Bateau Ivre*. A wild young man, his romantic feelings are freely indulged.

> James's music gave him not only the freedom of the oceans, the rolling of ships, the howling of gales, screeching seas, icy waves, strange, beautiful, rather disquieting flora and fauna, it gave him a more personal power of these phenomena, while at the same time making acceptable once for all the symbolism of the thing, the will to be abandoned and the will to be battered, the rising and sinking, the being blown about and the pride of riding great waves; the solitude, and awareness of force; the sob and the shout of men; the desire for power and the struggle to escape obliteration; the will to live and the will to die! (*I Bring Not Peace*, p. 203)

Such euphoric passages alternate with cutting under-graduate witticisms ('They're only harmful to gentlemen. They wouldn't hurt you in the least') and paradoxes ('Things happen, but the talk's the thing').

The Haldanes had in 1925 created a *cause célèbre* in the university. When Charlotte's first husband brought a divorce action, citing J. B. S. Haldane as co-respondent, the university disciplinary body asked him to resign his Readership in Biochemistry. Then he promptly brought an action in the civil courts against this body, and won it.[3] The Haldanes' household was therefore labelled 'advanced'. Moreover, J.B.S. became involved in politics, and subsequently, as a card-carrying Communist, and on the editorial board of the *Daily Worker*, grew doubly suspect. (But by that time both he and Lowry had left Cambridge.) It was at the Haldanes' home that Lowry met Martin Case, Haldane's assistant, with whom he went drinking in The Red Cow, a pub then put 'out of bounds' by the Proctors (the disciplinary officers of the university). Haldane himself held high office in a jolly drinking club, the Benskin Society, and on one occasion rescued Martin Case from a charge of dangerous driving by taking the chief witness, a nightwatchman, to drink in a pub just before the hearing came on, reducing him to incoherence. Afterwards, like a true Scot, Haldane sent Martin Case a bill for all the alcohol consumed by himself and the witness.[4]

Lowry stayed with the Case family on vacations, adopted the brothers as his own. After his publisher's copy of *Ultramarine* had been stolen, it was Martin Case who produced the rough notes, to put the book together again.

The Cases were all scientists; scientists cannot escape routine. Lowry did not follow orthodox paths, but he absorbed much at Cambridge. Moreover, the literary 'set' and Haldane's 'set' were the last in which he found any kind of substitute for the family life he so deeply needed, until he met the 'family' of the Dollarton fishing community. In chapter VI of *Under the Volcano*, the two brothers indulge in fraternal recollections of Cambridge, giving one of the lightest scenes of comedy in that tragic tale.

Lowry's relations with Charlotte Haldane are difficult to decipher after the lapse of years. He was infuriated by her book, but he makes Hugh boast slightly of a love affair with an older woman. Douglas Day suggests that Lowry was pursued by Charlotte (p. 138). His shyness was often protected by a blasé air; it is said that when at his wedding in Paris, the officials asked if he were willing to take Jan as his wife, he replied 'Ça va!' So later, he made rather a point of being superior about 'Chaddy Haldane's addled salon'.

Other novels came out of Lowry's Cambridge – Rosamund Lehmann's *Dusty Answer* (1927) and A. P. Rossiter's *Poor Scholars* (1932) depicting 'advanced' young people full of intense and contorted feelings. But much of the creative life of the time depended then, as always, on informal meetings between senior and junior members, or a few friends gathered in a room to talk or hear a paper. 'The talk's the thing.' Moore at the Moral Science Club, meditatively deflating a pompous speech – 'Oh! ... so you *think* so ... do you?' – or Virginia Woolf talking to an undergraduate club, and turning her talk to good account in *A Room of One's Own*, dozens of modest, ephemeral clubs in College, all encouraged Lowry's natural preference for literature as talk not print.[5] Many of the best public lectures of that time have never been published – such as T. S. Eliot's on the Metaphysical Poets, or I. A. Richards's on Eliot himself. The university was smaller, more informal, more self-contained. The poetry of the undergraduates, however, proclaimed the ubiquity of *The Waste Land*. Very direct imitation, 'possession' by a great contemporary, was no singularity of Malcolm Lowry. It is seen in Bronowski's 'October Casuistry'

We have come to the latter season of the year
when kingdoms tremble.

The triumphs go through the town
cohorted with the day-stubbled multitudes
with the old leaf's rusting,
charioted
to lay the summer's last dust aquarially.

Experiment, no. 2 (February 1929)

(In the same number Bronowski writes on symbolism, praising Cocteau, Aiken, O'Neill.) William Empson's *Seven Types of Ambiguity* also made a tentative first appearance in extracts in *Experiment*. Its emphasis on alternative meanings, deep-laid contradictions and paradoxical statement of opposites, though more analytical than anything of Lowry's, must have encouraged his multiplicity of levels, his development of mythopoeic suspensions. Among the books actually prescribed for the Tripos, Lowry would have found the *Fleurs du Mal* of Baudelaire, which gave direct intimation of the kind of structure he was later to develop. He quotes from Baudelaire in defence of *Under the Volcano*, in his letter to Jonathan Cape. To give the context of his glancing reference

La Nature est un temple où de vivants piliers
Laissent parfois sortir de confuses paroles;
L'homme y passe à travers des forêts de symboles
Qui l'observent avec des regards familiers.

Correspondances[6]

In his later works, as Lowry pointed out, the Symbolism became more explicit, the man more obviously building his own world from within. Yet the mixture of tragic and comic still remained, corresponding with the two moods, the menacing and the joyous, by which he was possessed. I. A. Richards's definition of tragic catharsis, 'Pity, the impulse to advance and terror, the impulse to retreat' stayed in Lowry's mind to reappear at a central moment in *Under the Volcano*, p. 251. Perhaps he remembered also Empson's discussion of Faustus' last speech 'Ugly hell, gape not! Come not, Lucifer!' where the commands seem to invite what they at the same time forbid.[7]

An extract from a gay Elizabethan comedy is placed at the start of that novel, along with the message, which by opening a book at random Laruelle receives from the dead Consul – his Faustian epitaph:

> Cut is the branch that might have grown full straight,
> And burned is Apollo's laurel bough,
> That sometimes grew within this learned man.
> Faustus is gone; regard his hellish fall . . .

Perhaps Lowry himself knew also those lines by Yeats which sum up his own double vision, in the work he left and the life he lived. They might provide his own epitaph

> A tree there is that from its topmost bough
> Is half all glittering flame, and half all green
> Abounding foliage moistened with the dew:
> And half is half and yet is all the scene.
> And half and half consume what they renew.
> ('Vacillation' II, from *The Winding Stair*)

Summary of Lowry's letter to Jonathan Cape
on *Under the Volcano*

This letter, a reply to the criticisms of Cape's Reader, was written in January 1946, and is printed in *Selected Letters*, pp. 57–88.

Lowry opens by defending his 'tedious' beginning, which gives 'the slow melancholy rhythm of Mexico itself' and establishes the 'terrain'. The book is 'deeper' than it looks, although the top level is carefully designed to hold the reader, for all its longueurs. As the writer's equipment is subjective, more a poet's than a novelist's, so the novel needs to be read more than once, as if it were a poem. The Reader's other objections are refuted: (ii) 'Weak characters.' There just isn't room for normal character drawing. (iii) 'Too much word spinning and stream of consciousness stuff.' This is thematic. (iv) 'Flashbacks tedious and unconvincing.' These are part of the 'churrigueresque'[1] structure. (v) 'Mexican local colour heaped on in shovelfuls' (though it is good). This is also necessary. A long defence against overlap with Charles Jackson's *The Lost Weekend* follows. *This* book is part of a projected trilogy. Its power has been tested by reading aloud; chapter vi has always succeeded as comedy.

Analysis of the structure

The twelve chapters are twelve blocks, each a unity in

133

itself but all are interrelated. Twelve is a significant number in many ways, especially it has cabbalistic significance.
The cabbala represents spiritual aspiration; the Tree of
Life with Light at the top and an abyss somewhere in the
middle. The Consul inhabits Qliphoth, the world of
shells and demons, represented by the Tree of Life in-
verted. The book is written on a variety of planes, with
something for every reader. Unlike Joyce, the author has
aimed at simplifying his complex effects. The novel can
be read as a story. It can be regarded as a symphony or
an opera.

It is hot music, a poem, a song, a tragedy, a comedy, a
farce, and so forth. It is superficial, profound, entertain-
ing and boring, according to taste. It is a prophecy, a
political warning, a cryptogram, a preposterous movie,
and a writing on the wall. It can even be regarded as a
sort of machine; it works too, believe me, as I have
found out!

It is concerned with the forces in man which cause him to
be terrified of himself. It is also concerned with guilt,
remorse, struggles towards the light, doom. The allegory
is that of the Garden of Eden. The drunkenness of the
Consul is used to symbolise the universal 'drunkenness'
of mankind, during the war, or during the period leading
up to it; his fate should be seen in its relationship to the
fate of mankind. The movement is that of a wheel with
twelve spokes, the motion being that of time itself [the
action takes just twelve hours, from 7 a.m. to 7 p.m.].

Chapter I. The Casino de Selva recalls the opening of
Dante's *Inferno*; the name is echoed in chapters VI, VII, XI,
the last being placed in a real wood. The scene is Mexico,
a place both paradisal and infernal. It is the Day of the
Dead [i.e. All Souls, 2 November]. Sympathy for the

Consul is established by the exposition of the Consul's and Laruelle's past life, and by the Taskersons. The horseman who is to reoccur throughout appears here. The movie symbolism represents the collective guilt of mankind and looks forward to the guilty hands of the *pelado* in ch. viii. The theme of Faustus is struck by the recovery of the Consul's copy of the play, and the letter found in it builds up sympathy for him; it is answered in ch. xii by Yvonne's letter. The motif of the Wheel is introduced at the end of this chapter.

(Note. In the cabbala, the misuse of magical powers is compared with the misuse of wine; the agonies of the drunkard are therefore analogous to those of the mystic who has misused his psychic powers.)

Chapter ii. The main story, exactly a year earlier; this chapter is a sort of bridge, dramatic, amusing.

Chapter iii. More exposition, and some thematic scenes; the Consul's impotence here balanced by his impotence with Maria in ch. xii. His 'vision' of the dead man is a true premonition of what occurs in ch. viii.

Chapter iv. Supplies movement, 'ozone', swiftness, understanding of Mexico; here Hugh's guilt balances the Consul's.

Chapter v. The book now 'fast sinks into the action of the mind, away from normal action'. The theme of the Waste Garden is that of the Garden of Eden, while Parián symbolises death. The rest is 'perfectly good clean D.T.s'.

Chapter vi. This is the heart of the book. Returning to Hugh, who is Everyman, and a new theme of guilt, nevertheless the situation is comic but with the Consul's magic books, the magic basis of the world itself is revealed. Perhaps if there is to be cutting, this chapter could take it.

Chapter vii. Seven is a magic number; this chapter first drafted in 1936 was rewritten five times. The 'usual thickness and obliquities, stray cards from the Tarot pack etc.'

in the scene on the Tower. The horseman reappears briefly. The Consul is presented with his last chance. 'Life is a forest of symbols, as Baudelaire said, but I won't be told you can't see the wood for the trees here!'

Chapter VIII. Here the book goes into reverse, or starts downhill, to the abyss. The bus ride and the encounter with the dying horseman represents Man himself, now dying – in another sense, he is the Consul too. In one sense the meaning is obvious, like a cartoon, a journalistic simplification; the top level carries on normally, but the wide political and religious significance should emerge. This chapter was the germ of the whole book [it exists in a separate short story version].

Chapter IX. This chapter was first written through Hugh's eyes, then the Consul's, then Yvonne's. It brings in Hope for the last time, which justifies the flashbacks. The Consul teeters between past and future, hope and despair, while Hugh, the other aspect of Everyman, is preposterously subduing those animal forces which later the Consul lets loose again. 'There are a thousand writers who can draw character till all is blue, for one who can tell you something new about hell fire. And I am telling you something new about hell fire.'

Chapter X. The advertisements for Tlaxcala are meant to be read with the eyes. Here the Consul is beginning to give way. The volcanoes are symbols of approaching war. If there are to be cuts, however, this chapter, with ch. VI, would be the best places to make them.

Chapter XI. The last to be written, it aims to pull out all the stops of Nature. It acts as contrast to ch. X and ch. XII and their horrors. Here Yvonne has to be killed in the dark wood, her end that of Marguerite in *Faust* (but people really are killed by horses in Mexico). Hugh is left singing drunkenly [in the earlier draft, Yvonne and Hugh are left making love in the wood].

136

Chapter xii. First written early in 1937, this is the best chapter. All strands are gathered up here; it balances chapter i. There is still some humour, which acts as bridge between naturalistic and transcendental. The deadly flat opening is essential. The esoteric elements are 'only a deep laid anchor anyway'; it is the fusion of many elements that makes the book. It is like a churrigueresque cathedral, yet it also has a severe classical pattern – for example, the Fascist brutes at the end can represent a revenge of the German submarine officers on the Consul. As the shape is that of a wheel, so the end returns to the beginning.

Two early stories from *The Fortnightly*,
the Leys School Magazine

A RAINY NIGHT

Somerset Maugham declares that the rain in tropical
regions has a depressing and demoralising effect upon the
inhabitants. It numbs the brain – this monotonous, almost
deafening hiss – causing people to do things that otherwise they would never dream of doing. Never having
been to the South Sea Isles, however, I can only take his
word for it. Still, here in comparatively unromantic
England I once committed a terrible, though I suppose,
quite excusable blunder, while it was raining.

Heavens! how it rained!

My excuse for blundering is obvious; my excuse for
writing this rather futile prologuette – if I may thus coin
a word – is perhaps not so obvious. However. . . .

It was in December. The morning had broken cold and
bleak, and gave every promise of rain. I was not dis-
pleased at this, for I had a long railway journey before
me – Yeovil to Liverpool, to be exact – (one has to run up
to Manchester and down again to get there – rather silly),
which normally is a very tiring and monotonous one.

However, when it is raining I confess to a sort of
infantile pleasure in listening to the rain pattering outside.
If it is fine on such occasions, I always feel that it is my
luck to have to spend a day travelling when I might be on
the golf links – in fact, every course of which it is possible
to obtain a brief cinematographic view as we pass inspires
me with a desire to take my clubs from the rack, jump out,

and have a game. On wet days things are very different. The flags on the greens, which are full of troubled pools, are so soaked as to have lost most of their flapping power. The bunkers are full of water. The fairways are punctuated with miniature lakes, with green shoots of grass appearing above the surface, looking as though the whole casual water (pardon the homely simile) was a bald man's head boasting still a few treasured hairs on top. The only signs of life are perhaps one disconsolate and half-soaked greenkeeper sheltering (he is not fully soaked because he has been sheltering most of the morning), a sodden sheep or two, maybe . . .

All this, when you have arranged for a game, is one of the most depressing spectacles on God's earth. When you cannot play, the irony of circumstances may make it one of the most comforting.

The various towns and villages which we passed through just before we reached Manchester looked slightly more repelling than usual. Moreover, when we reached that town it was dark. Outside, the rain having decided not to be half-hearted about things, lashed down as though the ground were a ceiling which it must penetrate at all costs. Everywhere sodden advertisements clung like wet rags. I caught glimpses of mackintoshed mothers and sons drinking coffee in waiting rooms, more people outside with umbrellas, more advertisements. . .

But it was cosy in my third class compartment. I seemed to be about the only person on the train, and with the lights on, a good magazine for company, and the home-coming at Liverpool to look forward to, I could not have been more contented.

In the meantime the rain was fairly sweeping against the window.

My host in the south, being one of those almost too obliging fellows, had insisted on having some sandwiches

139

made up for me for the journey. I did make a protest, as a matter of fact, but it was received in a 'No-no-my-dear-chap – no-trouble-whatever – no-trouble-whatever' sort of voice, so in the end I accepted his offer. But as they proved to be salmon, a fish which I abhor, I decided to have lunch on the train, and the sandwiches remained forgotten in my bag.

We were on the short run home to Liverpool.

With a feeling of boredom I threw down my magazine and edged myself into the corridor. I strolled up and down. The train appeared to be empty save for a little wizened, cross-eyed old man, who shivered in the corner of the corridor. I approached him.

'Why not come and sit down in the carriage? It must be rather cold out there,' I ventured.

'Aye not like sit in carriage in – these,' replied the man, indicating his clothing.

He spoke with a decided accent: what nation it belonged to I could not for the moment determine. He mumbled rather.

'Why, good lord, man,' I said, 'there's hardly another soul on the train. Anyhow, what if there were?'

'Py Jo! Aye forgat.' He spoke hurriedly. 'It very kind of you.' He came and sat down in my compartment.

'Not a bit; the railway company supply the seats. The obvious thing to do, as far as I can see, is to sit in them – having paid your fare. . . .'

'Ah! dat is it,' said he slowly; 'aye have not paid my fare. Your station-master – he pity me. . . . Py Jo! Aye forgat.'

'You forgat what?' I queried before I had time to realise the rudeness of the echo. 'Tell me the whole story,' I added.

I regarded my companion acutely (why must we always regard our companions acutely, by the way?). His cross eyes were glazed and seemed almost to be standing out of his head. His skin was greasy, where skin could be seen for dirt.

'Drink!' I thought: 'That's it. He does seem a curious man, and not English by the looks of him. German perhaps?' No, he didn't seem to be German. I put his age down at about sixty.

As if in answer to my question: 'Aye vas Svedish – Olivsen my name,' he said. 'Fireman on board *Tasmania*. Sailed from Manchester last night. Aye pick it up at Liverpool to-night. Olivsen – square-head name. Oder name Christofersen – vorse!'

'A fireman's life is pretty strenuous, isn't it?' I asked. 'How did you come to miss your boat, by the way?'

'Aye vas ill,' he replied simply.

For a moment I thought he was going to faint, but he seemed to recover himself. I was almost on the point of giving him a lecture on the distressing consequences of liquor, but I pulled up in time.

'Of course,' I added, keeping up the conversation, 'most of the ships are driven by oil now, aren't they?'

'Yes. Py Jo,' he said, 'Aye forgat.' Then, quietly and rather indistinctly: 'My life has been one tragedy.'

'Aye gat news on my last voyage that my kiddie. . . . he vas dead. Aye live in your country, you know. Aye hardly recover from news. Vhen I get back home, my vife – she has cleared.'

'Good lord!' I ejaculated, really sorry for the little fellow. 'Cleared? Do you mean she ran off with another man?'

'Vith oder man, no. Cleared – dead – like may kiddie. Py Jo!' he added brokenly. 'Aye hardly recover from news.'

'Oh!' I felt I couldn't say much else in the circumstances. Yet, though I hated myself for doing it, I almost added – 'and that's why you took to drink;' but I pulled myself up in time.

'Aye felt too ill to gat on boat last night,' he continued. 'She sail. Aye have no money to pick *Tasmania* up at Liverpool, where she spend the night. Aye vhalk to station and tell station-master may trouble. He have compassion and gat me ticket. That why I like not sit in compartment, as you say.'

'Well, if that's all your trouble.... Money....' I fingered my note case.

'No,' he broke out, holding up his hand: 'No! my pride already injured enough. I not take money from oder man. Dat station-master he very good, but if Aye had not been ill – vould sooner have vhalked to Liverpool – Py Jo! Aye forgat.' And he rambled on – a prolific talker, I thought; and, though I was ashamed of the thought, I felt that it was a good thing I hadn't given the money, for he would only have spent it on drink. Yet – he refused. Funny....

We were nearing the slums of Liverpool. A strong wind had risen. Through the blurred windows I could see a phantasmagoria of moving lights partly obscured by the driving rain which lashed up against the window in sudden whipping gusts. The wind whined in the telegraph wires. Slums – dirt – houses, in drab blocks of the same dull design; but there were lights in some of the windows betokening at any rate some vitality. It was more than poor Olivsen had. He pointed out the sight with a stubby forefinger belonging to a hand greased and grimed with indelible grime.

'It is more than Aye haf,' he said sadly, speaking my thoughts. He stopped.

'Drink,' I began; but I couldn't think quite how to go on, so I changed the subject. But, all the same, I felt pretty certain of the kind of illness that had prevented him from catching his boat.

142

We were nearing Central station then, plunging through the maze of tunnels which occur just outside the city.

'Now look here,' I said, suddenly magnanimous in the spirit of the season, 'we're getting near Liverpool now. It's a perfect beast of a night; you simply can't go dashing around catching boats. Suppose you come with me and I'll give you a job as a gardener or something at my place. I need one, by the way. And here's a couple of –' I never finished the sentence, though I had started fingering my note case again.

'Tank you, no!' he interrupted, holding up his hands. 'You are very kind. But I haf to do may duty by *Tasmania*. Aye sign on.'

'Good lord!' I began, 'they won't mind. Just –'

'Aye gat yob,' he continued, 'Aye hope keep yob. Aye take no money from anyone except for work Aye do. But you are very kind.'

'Well, if you won't –' I said, rather surprised, replacing my note case.

'Well, here's Central. Good-bye, old Swede.' And I stepped out into the corridor, threw open a window and engaged a porter almost in the same breath; and in the joy of seeing my wife, I forgot Olivsen entirely.

The latter still remained seated in the carriage. 'Old Svede!' he repeated to himself; 'that what he call me' (with a laugh). 'And Aye am only thirty-two!'

He half rose . . .

❖   ❖   ❖   ❖

That night the man whose business it is to go round the empty carriages, tapping the wheels, collecting the railway corporation tea cups and articles that have been left behind on the rack by the unwary, found a dead man in an empty compartment.

He called his mate, and the two of them carried the body into the waiting-room. The first man rang for a doctor. In the meantime, though it was quite late, a considerable crowd had gathered round. Eventually the doctor arrived, accompanied by a policeman.

The latter reproved the workmen for moving the body. The doctor made his examination, making the startling discovery that the man, who bore letters upon his person addressed to Christofersen Olivsen, had died of starvation. The body was removed to the mortuary and further investigations were postponed till the next day.

❋   ❋   ❋   ❋

At about the same time my wife was unpacking my kit-bag, laughing at my usual untidiness.

'Hello!' she remarked, as she noticed a certain parcel, 'you're absent-minded as well as untidy, now, my man. Why, you've forgotten your lunch!'

CAMEL

SATAN IN A BARREL

Pirated history, this story. You'll think you know what's coming. Mention a barrel or Satan in connexion with the judge of the Bloody Assize, and – bah! you know all about the incident. Old Jeffreys! What I don't know about Jeffreys, you say, is all written in the Lives of the Chancellors; what isn't in the Lives of the Chancellors is in Rafael Sabatini; and what isn't there is in the repertoire of every History master. There isn't, therefore, any scope for imagination concerning this man unless you tell blatant untruths. Well, why not? Untruths, especially when they might be true, are most satisfying. Besides, what, after all, do people know about him? Ben Jonson is reputed to

144

have seen the Romans and the Carthaginians fighting on his big toe in a dream. Mr Asquith said, 'Wait and See.' But did he? Did Ben Jonson? Who knows for certain? *Quaero ex te . . .*

* * * *

I feel perfectly certain that he was not there: I hunted everywhere: heaven was quite a small place. The psychology of dreams is an interesting study. Why was I, of all people, in heaven? A curtain at the back of my mind reefed up suddenly to reveal three stone walls, my mind being the fourth, a grating for a window, a hard bed, a rickety chair or two . . . A cell, ostensibly, in the Tower of London: most sinister; certainly an abstract creation of my fevered imagination, for I had never visited the place. Discovered – Judge Jeffreys and a warder. Highly dramatic. I braced myself in an ethereal stall . . . The warder was answering a question:

'I should have thought you were comfortable' – and he spoke in a voice like a cracked phonograph record.

'Comfort of body,' replied the judge slowly; 'yes; tolerably so. But of soul, definitely no. At the present moment my soul's in hell: at the end of a few days – or months – or years' (he gesticulated) . . . 'whatever it is, not only my soul but my body will be in hell.'

He spoke the last few words hurriedly and painfully, as if sentencing somebody whom he was loth to punish, but whom he wanted to be done with as quickly as possible. I remember this notion occurred to me at the time: it is most ironically inapt.

'I suppose you will say,' he continued, in much the same voice, 'that there is no difference. Yet I feel there is a very big difference . . . Do you, for instance, offer me any hope? . . . that is, if I improved?' he concluded lamely.

'I don't,' phonographed the warder. 'My reasons are as follows.' They followed.

145

Said the judge: 'There is no need to tell me all that: I know it already. You shouldn't touch a decomposed toad. You see if I am not past forgiveness.'

A clock, high up in the tower, struck ten. A voice whispered: 'You are not past forgiveness.'

'As I was saying,' went on the judge, 'before I was interrupted' (he was used to these voices), 'if I was not past forgiveness altogether, I might be able to redeem the past somewhat by prayer. At least I have my sane moments – *delirium tremens* has that quality – and I could pray. Couldn't I? Do you think yourself' – there was a pleading in his voice for the warder to say no – 'that I am past forgiveness? . . .' But the warder had gone.

'Surely,' sighed the judge, 'I'm not. And yet I've done a deal of mischief in my life . . . Oh! I must be. Yes, I'm past forgiveness. However . . . I haven't a friend in the world – except old Satan. How pleased old Satan must be – but then his gratification is a somewhat doubtful thing to be thankful for. No, not a friend. Pas un ami. Non est mihi amicus. Poor Latin that! Poor French too! However . . .' He paused, and then, 'I don't suggest for a moment that you deserve one.'

I felt rather sorry for him. A clock high up in the tower struck a quarter past ten. A voice said: 'You don't deserve one; but you have one all the same.' A kindly voice! it breathed good will! I could almost see it: it looked like violets in a mud-bank.

The judge started. He said: 'I don't believe it. Who are you? What do you mean by talking to me like this? Why are you always pestering me? Are you one of Satan's invisible messengers sent up from purgatory to goad me with fiery verbal pitchforks? Good, that! Very good for me. Ponder on it. If that is so, I'll tell you now, if you go away, I've done your work well – very well indeed! But go away.'

146

'I am,' replied the voice, 'the Voice of Grace. And, despite your rhetoric, you may still be saved.'

Poor voice! How futile it was to talk to Jeffreys.

The judge smiled sardonically. 'In the morning,' he said, 'I shall bribe the warder to kill me – nobody will know . . . If this monotony continues, I shall go mad.' He tore what remained of his hair to tear. Late evening drew on to blackest night: the stage darkened: Jeffreys watched the little pool of light cast through the dungeon bars on to the floor darken, and finally vanish as quickly as the sun obscured by galloping clouds on a dark day. Rain outside. The roads looked like canals of mud. Jeffreys and I could see something else too. His victims were parading past him in single file. Wind outside. The voice that looked like violets in a mud-bank was speaking above the wind. It said it was never too late – said it many times – until Jeffreys appeared hypnotised, and at last seemed to realise that this thing was advising him to pray. He said: 'It is ridiculous to pray. Praying is naught. Praying is canting, hypocritical. One goes down on one's knees and prays honeyed words to a Being you don't understand and believe in less.'

Then he said: 'I must pray. It is my last chance.'

The voice said: 'Pray, Jeffreys, pray!'

And he prayed. Prayed as he had presumably been taught to pray at his mother's knee – if she did teach him, which seems doubtful – prayed for forgiveness: prayed even for death, for at the moment he felt sure of deliverance afterwards.

'I am no worse,' he said, hoarsely, 'than the two who died with Thee, O Lord – and Thou saidst that one of them, because of his faith, should have a place in Paradise.'

'I see you know your Bible better than I should have thought . . .' said the voice. 'You are worse, much worse,

147

than he. But go on; pray, Jeffreys, pray: there is still hope for you if you hold to this state of mind.'

And so praying, he fell asleep, and it was not till the next day was well advanced that he awoke, having missed his breakfast. The judge felt a new man: all his thoughts of the night before about death at the hands of the warder were forgotten.

'If I stop drinking,' he said to himself, 'maybe I shan't die so soon after all – no! by Heaven! I shall not. And William may have mercy and release me. By Heaven! despite that sordid business in Wapping – despite my stone – perhaps I shall win through yet. Of course, they hate me here . . . Then I didn't, as a matter of fact, carry out my gallows-work enough for James . . . It was his fault. At least – no! it was my fault. My fault! I allow that. But there are other countries than England, other places than Wapping. Oh! I have been a sinful man, 'tis too true,' he sighed . 'But if only that chance is given me I shall preach good throughout the world. Somehow I really feel as though I had a friend or two.'

The warder entered with his mid-day meal – a very meagre bit of salmon – all he could digest.

'Good afternoon to you,' said the judge huskily.

The onlooked-for tone caused the warder a vague discomfort.

'A barrel of oysters has arrived for you – your Lordship. Marked "Colchester Oysters." Nothing else. No name, no sign.'

The judge did not conceal his joy. 'Oysters are my favourite dish,' he said slowly. 'Who can have thought of it? What extraordinary good luck! What a stroke of Providence! I shall sail the five seas on a snow-white yacht called Goodwill, which shall ride the seas like a bird!' he exclaimed, almost bursting with Arlenesque enthusiasm. 'That's what comes of being a true Christian'

148

(licking his lips); 'oysters have been my favourite dish since I was – oh! such a little boy.' He demonstrated.

Later the barrel was brought up to reveal, as history knows, not oysters, but a halter. Indeed, the cruel joke would have been quite as passable had there been oysters there, for there was no 'r' in the month: monotony, however, had probably killed knowledge of time in Jeffreys. Besides, that would have spoilt part of the irony of the jest.

'That,' laughed the warder, 'is a good joke. Tee-hee!' and his laughter, as he went out, echoed down the steps. More laughter from below.

The judge threw the halter angrily against the wall: then he stamped upon the rope, cursed it, and then said bitterly: 'I curse you, Jeffreys, vilest of men! I curse the sender of the barrel! I curse the halter! I curse Christianity! but above all, Fate, I curse you. I curse everything that you have given. Like Job, I curse the whole of my life. I fling everything back at your cruel face, senseless Fate! Be accursed, be for ever accursed! With my curses I conquer you – what else can you do to me? With my last thoughts I shout into your asinine ears – be accursed, be for ever accursed . . . My only trouble is that these are not my last thoughts. They can't be: I shall have to die! How can I die? I shall die of stone – or of a broken heart – or of drinking too much brandy. I have no appetite for healthy things: I hate even salmon now: a poached egg is too much for me. I don't want an appetite – I don't . . . Oh! but there's Christianity – the voices! They can't have been Christianity; must have been something else. Well, curse them . . . curse them!'

He looked into the barrel: 'I see the imprint of a cloven hoof,' he said. He paused.

'I curse Christ,' he declared simply. 'No I don't.' His voice lacked conviction. 'Yes, I do. I curse Christianity . . .'

Five hours galloped on. Light.

'Voices,' said Jeffreys. 'Oh! my voices, come again! Everything'll be right if you just come again, voices. I see great birds fighting and tearing – why, I know not. Voices! come again! I shall be saved. I'll be the Christian I've just been for a space – for the rest of my life . . . if those voices come again.'

But they came no more . . . The curtain crashed down. Nineteen clocks chimed eight unevenly.

CAMEL

NOTES

PROLOGUE

1 Oxford University Press, New York, 1973; London 1974.
2 Day, p. 323, quoting Cocteau; my translation.
3 For example, Schmidthüs, Lowry's teacher at Bonn (Day, p. 99); Nordahl Grieg, the Norwegian novelist.
4 It echoes the seaman's hymn 'Eternal Father, strong to save/ Whose arm doth bind the restless wave'. (For the verses see *Selected Poems*, p. 75.)
5 See below, p. 154 n. 28. The quotation is given by Day, p. 263, from the 1940 version.
6 *Arena*, London, 1949, Autumn issue (no. 2), 49–57. *Arena* was edited by John Davenport.
7 Lowry's transformations often involve *scale*: work is an elephant, the past a toy boat.
8 In a story written by his first wife, and cited by Day, Lowry squashes a puppy which he was bringing as a present; another story describes him actually stealing a kitten to give a child as a present.
9 Day, p. 62.
10 See above, p. 104. Harold Stoker is Russell Lowry.
11 Day, p. 62. His father remained for him the figure from his youth; he never imagined the septuagenarian with the bombed offices and suspended business who in 1944 died of cancer of the bowel.
12 B.B.C. Portrait of Malcolm Lowry, 1967.
13 Did he claim descent from the royal house of Scotland on the strength of Dunbar's improper little poem about the wooing of King James IV at Dunfermline?

> He wes ane lusty reid haird lowry,
> Ane lang taild beast and grit withal . . .

14 See Day, pp. 258–74 and pp. 316–50.
15 Dale Edmonds, '*Under the Volcano;* a Reading of the Immediate Level', *Tulane Studies in English*, xvi (1968), 63–105, considers: (1) Weight of the Past; (2) Salvage Operations – the

151

attempts to save the Consul; (3) A mosaic of Doom – the accumulating forces of destruction; (4) Drunk all morning . . . the alcoholic motif; and (5) Non se Puede Vivar sin amar, corresponding to Day's last level. Perle Epstein's reading is cabbalistic.

16 'Ghostkeeper' was published in *American Review*, 17 (Bantam Books, New York) in May 1973. A further collection of Lowry's work is announced there.

17 See, e.g. William H. New, *Malcolm Lowry*, Toronto: McClelland and Stewart, 1971, and *Articulating West*, Toronto: New Press, 1972, pp. 196–206.

CHAPTER 1: LOWRY'S ERIDANUS

1 For *Letters* see Bibliography.

2 Information from the family of the late Thomas McMorran, with whom Lowry stayed in youth. Cf. Day, p. 86.

3 First conceived in 1940 (*Letters*, p. 43) as a trilogy: by 1951, a sextet (*Letters*, p. 245).

4 These formed his 'original composition', a voluntary extra to the Tripos papers.

5 Summarised in Appendix A.

6 *Letters*, p. 373. See above, chapter 2, p. 43 for an account of this discussion.

7 *Under the Volcano*, p. 12; *Dark as the Grave*, p. 239.

8 *Letters*, p. 373; cf. *Blue Voyage*, p. 7. See above, p. 47.

9 Lowry file at the Leys School; private information; *Malcolm Lowry, the Man and His Work*, pp. 169–70.

10 Day, pp. 75–7 (he treats the allegations with scepticism). Cf. also *October Ferry*, pp. 20–3.

11 Day, pp. 66ff. recounts this and other stories (cf. above, pp. 26–7). Russell Lowry recollects that a temporary nursemaid, who momentarily replaced their trusty nanny, was dismissed after a week, for alleged beating of Malcolm with a bramble branch while taking him for a walk.

12 *Selected Poems*, p. 61.

13 Letter from Russell Lowry.

14 Nordahl Grieg, 1905–43, poet, playwright, novelist, the most famous Norse writer of his generation. Cf. above, pp. 46–7.

15 *Letters*, p. 251. As a pretentious, grandiose vulgarity 'Clarence' was mortifying; a Shakespearean joke passed it off (see *Richard III*, Act I), for the significance of 'Lowry', see above p. 9. 'Malcolm' (servant of Colum) he liked.

16 As a lad, Arthur Lowry did one job by day, another in the evening; his twelve brothers and sisters were joined by thirteen orphan children of an uncle who had died young; and all

these were eventually helped by the elder Lowry. The violence of Malcolm's repudiation did not conceal that he had a strong respect and affection, mixed with fear, for his father. (Day, pp. 62–5; reaction under psychiatric treatment, pp. 25–6.)

17 Lowry's grandmother lived to be ninety (Day, pp. 58–9 seems to have been misinformed about Lowry's grandparents).

18 *Letters*, p. 333 (cf. also pp. 255, 261, 263). Lowry accepts clairvoyance (p. 265). Conrad Aiken mentions his 'sixth sense mysticism' (*Ushant*, p. 224). Compare also *Hear Us O Lord*, p. 127 and cf. above, p. 29 and p. 117. Lowry's landlady at his latest home, Ripe, believed he had second sight and knew he was going to die (Day, p. 39).

19 His banishment to prep. school at seven would be an aggravation of his anxiety. For the effects of maternal deprivation, see John Bowlby, *Child Care and the Growth of Love* (1953). Note that in *Under the Volcano* both Geoffrey and Hugh are orphaned out in India – which was where Mrs Lowry went with her husband thus 'orphaning' her youngest son.

20 Day quotes from these reports (pp. 82–4); they are an intensified form of family chaffing. Very late in his life Lowry picked up the tone again (see above, p. 95, and p. 112) and he wrote an unpublished story 'Enter One in Sumptuous Armour' in which a schoolboy is enabled to face the ordeals of his school by learning to play goal at hockey. (The title refers to Shakespeare's *Troilus and Cressida*, v. 6.)

21 In the absence of father, Wilfrid extracted the modest sum to pay the fares for a visit to France with the school hockey team.

22 Day reports this, p. 304.

23 *Letters*, p. 151: 'My brother liberated the Channel Islands single-handed without a shot being fired, there being nobody there apparently to shoot.' Wilfrid who served in the Artillery, was awaiting the embarkation that never came when he wrote to Malcolm.

24 *Letters*, p. 240. Stuart Lowry had learnt it as a boy from a minstrel troupe in the Happy Valley at Llandudno; at the Leys School, where new boys were expected to entertain their house with a song, he used it and taught it to Wilfrid, who in turn taught it to the others.

25 The Lighthouse (the Farolito) and the Forest are powerful elements in the composite scene of this book; but the landscape is literally precise and the scene is misunderstood if it is misread (as by Perle Epstein in *The Private Labyrinth of Malcolm Lowry* (New York, 1969), pp. 67–9). 'Hell Bunker' is a well-known hazard at Hoylake.

26 i.e. 'holed-out' in one shot – this is called 'an Eagle'.

27 The burning of his house at Dollarton was the worst thing that ever happened to him, as Lowry told a friend.

153

28 Cf. above, p. 7. Day, p. 233, quotes the ending of a story written by Lowry's first wife, Jan Gabrial, which describes their parting in fictional terms: 'the boat that was Michael had slipped its moorings in her life, and was even now putting out to the darker sea to which she could not follow him' (published Sept.–Oct. 1946).

29 Cf. *October Ferry*, p. 210, for the 'battering of a second consciousness' at a moment of sharp change of mood. The implications of this attitude are developed above, chapter 6, pp. 82–3.

30 *Under the Volcano*, pp. 122–6, 352.

31 Compare the poem 'Thirty five mescals in Cuautla' (*Selected Poems*, p. 35) dated 1937. 'On the pictured calendar set to the future, / The two reindeer battle to death . . .'

32 The identification is actually made in the late story 'Ghostkeeper', where the hero walking on the beach of Vancouver Bay thinks himself back in New Brighton, England. Shortly afterwards he goes to see a film which was taken at New Brighton, his birthplace.

33 With 'Gin and Goldenrod' and *October Ferry* (originally designed as a short story) they form the Eridanus Quartet, to apply a term Lowry would have found relevant. This depicts a gradual movement out of this primal Eden, and an encroachment of the world. The equation of a primal landscape with early experience of mother's body is too familiar a notion in psychiatry to need comment.

34 Liverpool City Library – MS 1069 [Local Records]. It does not appear that this artless writer, whose name, James Ward, appears in *Ultramarine*, had actually read any of Lowry's books.

35 *Hear Us O Lord*, p. 255. The names of two men who made the path; but the symbolism is stressed also.

36 Among stories mentioned in November 1950 is 'The Course' – a story about Hoylake golf course and another about visiting a puritanical English home (*Letters*, p. 216). Neither is with the Lowry MSS at British Columbia. But 'Enter One in Sumptuous Armour', an unpublished tale, opens on the Wirral, moving to a public school. This story was extensively annotated and revised at quite a late date. The gardener is called Henrik Ghostkeeper. 'The Course' could be an alternative title.

CHAPTER 2: ULTRAMARINE

1 I have developed the theme of journeys in the final chapter of my *Literature in Action* (Chatto and Windus, 1972) with particular reference to Lowry.

2 One of the Dollarton jokes was incorporated in the seamen's talk eventually, as Mrs Lowry records in her preface.

3 *Letters*, pp. 264–5. Eliot and Aiken were at Harvard together.

4 He claims to have been sent down for failing his 'Mays' (first year examinations) and various peccadilloes, whereas in the Cambridge sequence in *Under the Volcano* Hugh Firmin only risks this catastrophe, having been advised by the lamp-trimmer on his freighter to get what he can out of the 'poxing place'.

5 Conrad Aiken claimed to have a typed copy, presumably the one with annotations. Cf. p. 129.

6 Lowry's father when he first left home insisted that he collect his allowance in person, afterwards arranging for it to be paid through someone who would be responsible for Lowry and report to him. In 1938, the elder Lowry's lawyers appear to have rescued Malcolm from his appalling plight in Mexico, but in the U.S.A. Arthur Lowry's legal agent had Malcolm declared incompetent (i.e. he held something like a power of attorney). It was he who got Lowry up to Canada just before divorce proceedings began; and Lowry had to stay there. (See Day, pp. 246–58.)

7 'The dithering crack of two boulders hurtling together under the sea' (*Blue Voyage,* p. 80; in the short story 'Economic Conference 1934' this phrase is used again); 'He thinks I'm a bird in a tree' (*Ushant,* p. 35); 'Merry laughter. "Married, does he say? No, siree, Bob. When Demarest marries they'll fire cannon and blow up the ship"' (*Blue Voyage,* p. 268).

8 *See Letters,* pp. 275–6 and *Ultramarine,* pp. 25–6. In the first version, the hero was *more* cowardly; he was not restrained by his friends from diving. Aiken's feat was to climb a telegraph pole and rescue a kitten. (*Letters,* p. 275)

9 The earliest piece of *Ultramarine* had appeared in *Venture,* no. 6 (1931) and dealt with Lowry's fear of syphilis, a subject also appearing in the novel of Grieg. The humiliating inadequacy of Lowry's attempts to satisfy a Japanese girl, recorded by his shipmates, are reflected in the Yokohama brothel.

10 See above, pp. 11–12. The correspondences strengthened Lowry's belief in universal patterns of an inexplicable and unpredictable kind. This was part of the personal mysticism he developed.

11 Hugh's aunt had said to a newspaperman as he went off, 'No silk cushions for Hugh' (*Under the Volcano,* p. 163), a phrase that in 1927 the newspapers attributed to Lowry himself at the start of his voyage (*Malcolm Lowry, the Man and His Work,* p. 56). *s.s. Pyrrhus* was a regular Blue Piper (not a tramp steamer) and her Master came from West Kirby very near Lowry's home at Caldy.

12 See *October Ferry,* p. 236; compare *Letters,* p. 262. See above, p. 101. Details like the hero's double registration for this ship are repeated, but where 'A' is saved, the later young man is drowned.

155

13 *Letters*, p. 263. The coincidence of names and places, when these are ships, ports, etc., hardly bear the weight put on them. Grieg was not thinking of going to Lowry's Cambridge to read the Elizabethans but to Oxford to read Rupert Brooke. This habit of identification, however, in a freer and more imaginative form produces the echoes and reflections discussed above, pp. 41–2.

14 See James Stern, 'Malcolm Lowry, a first impression', *Encounter*, vol. xxix, no. 3 (Sept. 1967) and Day, pp. 121–2. It is not clear whether Lowry found Grieg in Oslo or in a mountain hut.

15 See *Letters*, pp. 63, 442. Mrs Lowry said the book was to be 'if not in its original form, certainly in its original spirit and conception of meaning to the whole'. See above, p. 101.

16 He claimed to have been there voluntarily but was not (Day, p. 196). This story was originally called *The Last Address*, then *Swinging the Maelstrom*. See David Benham, 'Lowry's Purgatory', *Malcolm Lowry, the Man and His Work*, pp. 56ff. Day also compares the three versions of this tale (pp. 209–12).

17 Sigbjørn Lawhill is the hero's name in the first draft, Bill Plantagenet in the second. The *Lawhill* was a windjammer that survived more disasters than any ship afloat (p. 50). 'Plantagenet' reflects Lowry's own first name 'Clarence', since the original Duke of Clarence was a Plantagenet.

18 The desolate scene at Liverpool Pier Head on a windy day is caught in Lowry's first tale, 'Goya the Obscure' by the precise cry of the newsboys' *'Yacko! Last Echo, Exprey!'* and the sound of the dock railway bell 'ylang, ylang'. It is built into *Ultramarine* (p. 73), where the final tragic story of the newsboy who collapses and dies (see p. 200) links on again, verbally, with the death of the Consul in *Under the Volcano* (see below, p. 157, n. 12).

19 This storm recalls Rimbaud's *Bateau Ivre; Une Saison en Enfer* is quoted at the opening of the story. Garry is compared with Rimbaud at one point.

20 Possibly *Inferno*, Canto xxxii; but here the idea is purgatorial, one sinner helping another.

CHAPTER 3: UNDER THE VOLCANO

1 'Pity the impulse to advance and terror the impulse to retreat' is I. A. Richards's rewording of Aristotle's doctrine of catharsis in tragedy.

2 *Letters*, pp. 197–201.

3 *Letters*, pp. 177, 258. Day gives a mocking commentary of some academic 'drudgery' before offering his *Gestalt* explanation, and giving five approaches (pp. 320–50).

4 *Letters,* p. 66; repeated also in the preface to the French edition, written by Lowry.
5 *Letters,* p. 200.
6 'Thirty-five Mescals in Cuautla', *Selected Poems,* p. 35.
7 *Letters,* p. 73.
8 *Letters,* p. 80. All these quotations are from the long explanatory letters to Jonathan Cape. See Appendix A for summary.
9 Lowry once seized the hand of a man named Brockenshaw who had stolen his friend's mistress, and held it on a red-hot stove. The Consul is accused of putting some German prisoners into the ship's furnace.
10 Also the age of Stuart Lowry when he returned in 1924 from Texas, wearing like Hugh colourful Texan outfits.
11 Christ the Lighthouse.
12 The Consul's last moment of being 'He felt the life slivering out of him like liver' (p. 374) echoes, with the ideas of climbing, the last pages of *Ultramarine,* the death of the newsboy (p. 158). The Consul's phrase for coincidence 'correspondence between the subnormal world and the abnormally suspicious' (p. 140) is repeated in *October Ferry* (p. 320) with an opposite sense.
13 See above, pp. 71–2.
14 Lowry liked to give such presents: Mrs Wilfrid Lowry remembers his schoolboy gifts.
15 Day rejects this idea, which Lowry later repeated to John Davenport and James Stern (see *Selected Letters,* p. 11, p. 29; Day, p. 237).
16 See chapter v, pp. 82ff.
17 See Paul G. Tiessen, 'Malcolm Lowry and the Cinema' in *Malcolm Lowry the Man and his Work,* pp. 133–44. Cf. p. 31 above.

CHAPTER 4: STORIES, 1946–56

1 See above, chapter 1, p. 26.
2 Lowry subsequently made two murderous attacks on his wife, the first about two years after the Mexican trip (Day, p. 402).
3 This is much more crudely and explicitly treated in the recently published 'Ghostkeeper', a late story (*American Review,* 17 May 1973).
4 The harsh review of Jacques Barzun with the phrase 'And while imitating Joyce, Dos Pasos and Sterne, he gives us the heart and mind of Sir Philip Gibbs' (see *Letters,* p. 143). This is quoted twice in *Dark as the Grave* – attributed to a publisher's reader (pp. 142, 249). For further consideration of the effects of writing see above, pp. 82–3.
5 An American named Bousfield (Day, p. 246 and p. 352).
6 In the first draft of *La Mordida* the hero is named Martin

Trumbaugh; in the second draft he has become Sigbjørn Wilderness. His adventures combine some features of Lowry's visit to Mexico with his first wife and some of his visit with his second wife, in particular the final episodes; but this part is fragmentary and unshaped.

7 The date was ominous for Lowry, being the anniversary of a friend's death (see p. 114).

8 *Flying Enterprise* was the ship on which Capt. Kurt Carlsen and Kenneth Dancy battled so heroically (see Ralph Barker, *Against the Sea*, Chatto, 1972).

9 P. 44. See the last chapter for the explanation of this allusion, p. 113.

10 See Geoffrey Durrant, 'Death in Life; Neo-Platonic Elements in 'Through the Panama', *Malcolm Lowry, the Man and his Work*, pp. 42–55.

11 See W. H. New, 'Lowry's Reading' in *Malcolm Lowry, the Man and his Work*, p. 127.

12 Roderick MacGregor Fairhaven is named from Poe's Roderick Usher, as well as Scott's outlaw (*Lady of the Lake*) and Fairhaven the town near New Bedford where Melville set his scene. A good analysis of all the significance of proper names is given in William H. New, *Malcolm Lowry* (Toronto, 1971).

13 The elephant is somehow connected with the deceased Mother Drumgold, who in his infancy had given Cosnahan a grey suède elephant, while he had brought her a lapis lazuli elephant as a present from his first voyage. For Lowry's strange encounter with two elephants see Day, p. 153.

14 His brother Russell states that Malcolm received the income of the five-figure trust set up for him in 1938. His father's will which was so complex as to lead to Chancery rulings, left his estate to his widow for life, and then to the four sons Malcolm's share being in trust. Evelyn Lowry died intestate.

15 Cf. *Letters*, p. 332, the water-diviner, Aylmar. The water-diviner is an image for the psychic powers.

16 See the last pages of *Ultramarine* where Hilliot wins over his messmates by telling them a story of how the elephant got out in a storm and released all the other animals and they ran the ship – a fantastic dream story.

17 The Isle of Man, traditionally a home of sorcery for other Celts, and home of the Dead, used to have one or two people who still spoke a little Manx Gaelic secretly at home. For a Liverpool child it is familiar as a holiday haunt, and the Lowry children went there. All the names listed are Manx.

18 See John Rickman, *Selected Contributions to Psycho-analysis*, ed. Scott, 1957, especially p. 159. Cf. Herman Hesse's *Steppenwolf* – Lowry once signed himself ' Malcolm von Steppenwolf'.

CHAPTER 5: OCTOBER FERRY TO GABRIOLA

1 An aeolian harp is a wind harp, i.e. the unity in this book issues from the spirit *(pneuma)* – it is not explicit or formal.
2 'The Bravest Boat', 'Gin and Goldenrod', 'The Forest Path to the Spring'.
3 'These men of Inishmaan seemed to be moved by strange archaic sympathies with the world. Their mood accorded itself with wonderful fineness to the suggestions of the day', J. M. Synge, 'The Aran Islands' *(Prose,* ed. Alan Price, 1966, p. 142).
4 The central discussion in *Dark as the Grave* between Wilderness and Dr Hippolyte (chapter vii), see above (pp. 69, 73), pp. 102–3.
5 See *Letters,* p. 267 for one scheme.
6 An artist whose works were known to Lowry, the Norwegian painter Edward Munch, also hoarded his paintings, refusing to sell and continuously repainting the same subjects. This could be defined psychologically as the refusal to reify a process.
7 Day indicates the tremendous importance of the pier as a vital symbol (pp. 35–6).
8 Rivera's fresco in Mexico City shows Christ at the controls of an aeroplane, among the capitalists.
9 Nathaniel Hawthorne's 'Ethan Brand' in *The Snow Image,* 1851, tells of a man who committed the unforgivable sin of splitting his mind and heart. The savage taunting jests with which Ethan Llewelyn recollects goading his friend derive from such a split.
10 Yellow is the colour of the executioner's shed, stressed here and there (pp. 49, 287, 299). For the film *Outward Bound,* see 'Through the Panama', *Hear Us O Lord,* p. 35.
11 All is 'explained' in an occult work by Charles Fort, *Wild Talents* (1932) which Llewelyn finds and reads. For Fort, see above, p. 6, pp. 118–19.
12 See above for another attack on the novel, p. 56. At one point Lowry said he thought *October Ferry* would have been better expressed in ten short poems.
13 *October Ferry,* p. 207. But 'once a month he likes to get pretty tight'. This passage is the most direct fictional statement of alcoholic recovery and relapse.
14 'In the current', p. 320; at this point a phrase from *Under the Volcano* (p. 40) reoccurs about correspondence between the subnormal world and the abnormally suspicious. For the story of the Calgary farmer who found his brother struck dead, with his team of horses, see *Dark as the Grave,* p. 240, *October Ferry,* p. 274.
15 P. 146; compare the verse 'No Still Path' *(Selected Poems,*

p. 50): 'There is no path, there is no path at all / Unless perhaps where abstract things have gone / And precepts rise and metaphysics fall / And principles abandoned stumble on.'

16 However, at one point he is described in hospital in terms of Lowry's own experience (p. 190, see *Letters*, p. 368). Lowry has got himself – a boy – into the picture, perhaps.

17 Ethan is supposed to have been a captain in Intelligence during the war. The collective effort 'reminded him of the whole overstuffed stupid world doing eternally what it was told by its gruesome parents and groaning and straining for ever on a pot; the war effort' (p. 109).

18 This seems the moment to recall I. A. Richards's first meeting with Lowry. I. A. Richards describes how he went to a bullfight in Spain with Lowry and Conrad Aiken and Aiken's 'Lorelei', bearing a bottle of brandy in case the lady should be overcome by the blood; how at one point Lowry murmured solicitously 'A little brandy' to Richards who unsuspectingly passed the bottle which Lowry then emptied himself.

19 Ethan finds the Consul's lost golf ball, the Zodiac Zone (p. 113). Cf. above, p. 31; he is mistaken by the boys at his son's school for a spy (pp. 105, 120). The ritual drinking, the use of films to point these themes, the burning wheel, and the war in Europe offer pervasive correspondences between the two books.

20 For the story of Lowry's lost book, see also p. 48 and *Letters*, pp. 255–7, 261–3.

21 See above, pp. 113–15, for the sequel.

22 See pp. 87, 274, 330. The boy gaily announces the burning of the house; Llewelyn uses the phrase to greet the man he saved from a murder charge; Jacqueline discovers the heavenly omen of the shower of meteors.

23 *October Ferry*, pp. 168, 267; *Letters*, p. 269; *Hear Us O Lord*, p. 18. The boy was to be executed in a disused lift shaft, painted yellow, like the ferry. This boy and Garry in *Lunar Caustic* might reflect Lowry's sense of guilt for 'imaginary murder'.

CHAPTER 6: CHARON'S FERRY

1 See above, p. 76.

2 *Letters*, p. 339.

3 See above, pp. 22, 38.

4 From 'Trinity', a late poem (*Selected Poems*, p. 74). The arcades are the Goree Piazzas, where local legend, quite untruly, had it that slaves were formerly chained on their way to America (*Ultramarine*, p. 73).

5 At the outward extremity of the Liverpool docks, Bootle represents ultimate disgust in a statement attributed to M-lc-lm

L-wry in the St Catharine's College Magazine for Lent Term 1932, under the heading 'Great Minds at Work': 'He was a porter at Bootle. He felt like Hell. He always feels like Hell. He owes me £5.'

6 'I name this ship . . . God bless her and all who sail in her.'

7 Two ferry boats went to Dunkirk. One was sunk in the Mersey in the blitz.

8 Here is the flaying and perhaps the crucifixion of the 'Autopsy' (see above, p. 22). The 'ordeal' of joining the Wolf Cubs must have been at about eight years old; the 'ordeal' of joining the Leys School at fourteen was met by the Wibberlie Wobberlie song (above, p. 30).

9 One of his interventions in a school debate, on whether self-made men are inferior to public school boys, may represent a defence of his father.

10 From the Leys School 'file'. See also Day, p. 80.

11 Clare's 'poor snail' comes in *Summer Images*, a poem about the idyllic life of boyhood: 'Frail brother of the morn / That from the tiny bents and misted leaves / Withdraws his timid horn / And fearful vision weaves.' The verse is mockingly re-called later: *Ultramarine*, p. 54.

12 See above, pp. 8, 22. While at prep. school it was thought that he was indifferent to Wilfrid's triumph in playing for England. Later another schoolmate thought him rather too conscious of not being as good as his brother and 'trying to make up for it by head-down energy, bull-in-a-china-shop tactics'.

13 'Der Tag' may commemorate an occasion which Russell Lowry thinks of considerable significance, in which Malcolm was beaten for a fault in composition with excessive severity by a master who evidently lost his temper. His brother thinks this may have converted Malcolm from sport (which this master had encouraged him to try) to the attacks on sport that began when he was about sixteen.

14 See above, p. 45. One of Lowry's later dangerous exploits was the rescue of a trapped bird (*Letters*, pp. 336–7).

15 See above, pp. 37, 45, 55. Lowry's hands and feet and, according to the sailor, other members, were unusually small (cf. Day, p. 25).

16 See *Letters*, pp. 255–66, and above p. 48. It may be compared with account of Christopher Isherwood in *Lions and Shadows* (see Epilogue).

17 Fitte was living in one of the most expensive lodgings for St Catharine's in Trumpington Street, and the Manciple thinks Lowry also lived there. The boy's father spoke of his son's exaggerated sense of shame. Fitte had spent wildly, had visited undesirable acquaintances in London, had wanted to leave the university. He was probably being blackmailed. Charlotte

Haldane gives an imaginative account of this in *I Bring Not Peace* (1932) (see above, pp. 127–8). The suicide appears in other unpublished works of Lowry (see Day, pp. 137, 142–3), where the victim is named Wensleydale.

18 Cordwainer (shoemaker) suggests punningly a wanderer and an exile, and a hanged man. In *Dark as the Grave* Sigbjørn Wilderness tries to hang himself.

19 Cf. *Ultramarine*, p. 106. For a very late incident of Lowry's violent taunting of a friend see Day, p. 462.

20 In *October Ferry* the book cited is a later work by Fort, *Wild Talents* (1932).

21 Again Perle Epstein misreads the scene because she does not follow the literal level of the mnemonic sequence (*The Private Labyrinth of Malcolm Lowry*, p. 90).

22 One of the most touching, 'Kingfishers in British Columbia' (*Selected Poems*, p. 63) describes how the bird 'comes like a left wing / three-quarter cutting through toward / the goal in sun-lamped / fog at Rosslyn Park at half / past three in halcyon days'. Here the 'red fog at sun-rise' and a bird's beauty recall a winter Rugby game of boyhood, and Wilfrid cutting in to shoot.

23 *Hypocrisy, from* 'Some Poems', *Malcolm Lowry the Man and his Work*, p. 95.

24 Lowry's sense of being 'watched', his fear that his own life was being written by some higher power has much in common with John Wesley's view on special providence. To his father Lowry apparently continued to use religious imagery (Day, p. 297), and in particular he did not hesitate to use the life of Christ as a mirror for his own Gethsemanes and Golgothas.

EPILOGUE

1 P. 121. This prophecy is so far from being fulfilled that fifty years later, and aged eighty, Richards is about to publish his own third book of poems. Much of the mood of this time may be gathered from the *Essays In Honour of I. A. Richards*, ed. Reuben Brower et al. (O.U.P. 1973).

2 The Haldanes lived in Roebuck House, Old Chesterton; in *Ultramarine*, Hilliot says 'I pursued women from street to street, from lamp to lamp, from Petty Cury to Old Chesterton, always remaining a virgin. When they spoke to me I ran away.'

3 See Ronald Clark, *J.B.S.; Life and Work of J. B. S. Haldane*, Hodder and Stoughton, 1968, chapter 4; 'A Geneticist in the Headlines'. Subsequent chapters supplied me with material on Haldane and Case.

4 During the Second World War and just prior to the war, Martin

Case worked in some very hazardous experiments with Haldane, designed to effect the rescue of men trapped in submarines. See Ronald Clark's book. But Lowry of course knew nothing of this secret work, nor perhaps of Haldane's work for Spanish loyalists in 1935–6.

5 Lowry's best piece of work for Tom Henn was on oral literature – medieval ballads and sea shanties. His thesis about continuous creations (see above, p. 87) implies *spoken* literature.

6 *Selected Letters*, p. 78 (end of defence of chapter vii; cf. also Appendix A, p. 136 above).

7 W. Empson, *Seven Types of Ambiguity*, Chatto, 1930, p. 261. 'There is *no* stress, as a matter of scansion, on the negatives, so that the main meaning is a shuddering acceptance . . . one cannot recite *Ugly hell, gape not* as a direct imperative like "Stop gaping there!" ' Compare the Consul's last words to Hugh and Yvonne. 'I choose . . . Hell . . . because . . . I like it. I love Hell. I can't wait to get back there. . . .' (p. 316).

APPENDIX A

1 An extreme and intricate form of late baroque, highly decorated, found in Mexico.

BIBLIOGRAPHY

LOWRY'S WORKS

PROSE

Under the Volcano. First published 1947, Jonathan Cape (London); Rayner and Hitchcock (New York); Penguin Books, 1962.

Ultramarine. Revised edition, with note by Margerie Bonner Lowry, Jonathan Cape, 1962; Penguin Books. (Original edition 1933.)

Hear Us O Lord from Heaven Thy Dwelling Place. Philadelphia: Lippincott, 1961; Jonathan Cape, London, 1961. Also in Penguin Books. Contains seven tales, two published in Lowry's lifetime.

Lunar Caustic. First appeared in *Paris Review*, VIII. 29 (Winter–Spring, 1963). Jonathan Cape, London, 1968 (Cape Editions) with a prefatory note of Conrad Knickerbocker. Novella.

Dark as the Grave wherein my Friend is Laid. Edited by Douglas Day and Margerie Bonner Lowry. New York; New American Library, 1968; Jonathan Cape, London, 1969. Also in Penguin Books.

October Ferry to Gabriola. Edited by Margerie Bonner Lowry. New York: World, 1970; Jonathan Cape, London, 1971. Also in Penguin Books. A section entitled 'The Element Follows You Around, Sir!' appeared in *Show Magazine* (March 1964), 45–103.

VERSE

Selected Poems. Edited by Earle Birney with the assistance of Margerie Bonner Lowry. San Francisco: City Lights Books, 1962. Contains about a third of the surviving verses.

LETTERS

Selected Letters. Edited by Harvey Breit and Margerie Bonner Lowry. Philadelphia: Lippincott, 1965; Jonathan Cape, London, 1967.

UNCOLLECTED PROSE

'The Light that Failed Not'. *The Leys Fortnightly*, XLIX (13 March 1925), 'Travelling Light', XLIX (8 June 1925), 'The Blue Bonnet', L (9 October 1925), 'A Rainy Night', L (23 October 1925),

Bibliography

'Satan in a Barrel', L (12 February 1926), 'The Repulsive Tragedy of the Incredulous Englishman', L (4 June 1925). (There are also a number of verses in *The Leys Fortnightly*.) Lowry's pen name, Camel, an extension of his initials C.M.L., has been ascribed to his housemaster and his brother, but may carry a derisive reminder of his already noticeable inability to go without drink. Other boys called him 'Lobs', as did the seamen.

'Port Swettenham', *Experiment*, no. 5 (Cambridge, February 1930).

'Goya the Obscure', *The Venture*, no. 6 (Cambridge, June 1930).

'Punctum Indifferens Skibet Gaar Videre', *Experiment*, no. 7 (Cambridge, Spring 1931). Published in *Best British Short Stories of 1931*, as 'Seductio ad Absurdum'.

'On Board the West Hardaway' (*Story Magazine*, III, October 1933) is another version of 'Port Swettenham'.

'In Le Havre', *Life and Letters*, x, 55 (July 1934).

'Hotel Room in Chartres', *Story*, v (26 September 1934).

'Economic Conference, 1934', *Arena*, no. 2 (Autumn 1949).

'Bulls of the Resurrection', *Prism International*, v. 1 (Summer 1965).

'Ghostkeeper', *American Review*, 17 (May 1973).

A short story version of *Under the Volcano* was first published in *Prairie Schooner*, XXXVII, no. 4 (Winter 1963–4) and has been several times reprinted since.

There are more verses in *Arena*, no. 2 and in *Malcolm Lowry, the Man and his Work*, ed. George Woodcock, Vancouver, 1971.

MANUSCRIPTS

The Special Collections Department of the Library of the University of British Columbia, Vancouver 8, B.C., contains the Lowry MSS from his homes in Dollarton and in Ripe, Sussex, including letters, notes and the MS of the unpublished novel *La Mordida* (419 pp. plus notes), 'The Ordeal of Sigbjørn Wilderness' (160 pp.) and a number of fragmentary short stories. There is also a political essay, 'Halt! I protest!'

I am indebted to Miss S. M. Gillies for the following summary of the MS of *La Mordida*:

'There is a pencil MS, very incomplete and in this the hero is Martin Trumbaugh. There is also a typed MS, 45 chapters – some of the later ones only a page or two – and in this the hero is Sigbjørn Wilderness. The first four chapters, about one third of the whole, describe the journey to Acapulco, the mood being joyful, though punctuated by past fears and troubles. In Chapter v trouble threatens them with the 50 pesos fine (*La Mordida*) and deportation. Then comes a kind of parenthesis, most of chapter VI, headed "A Dream about a voyage from New Orleans to Haiti". From then on the nightmarish Kafkaesque quality increases, with the theme of imprisonment underlined and more drunkenness till eventually the American frontier is reached. All the last part is sketchy and interrupted by notes from the author or Margerie saying this must be changed or developed. There are also railway and bus time-tables and paper clippings.'

The short stories include 'China' (7 pp.); 'Enter One in Sumptuous Armour' (32 pp.); 'In the Black Hills' (5 pp.); 'June 30th 1934' (21 pp.); 'Noblesse Oblige' (11 pp.); 'Nocturnal Genius' (11 pp.); 'Portrait of the Conquistador' (9 pp. handwritten); 'Shadow' (17 pp.); 'Tramps' (8 pp.), and 'We're all Good Ducks Here' (9 pp.).

According to the prefaces, about two-thirds of the Letters are in print but only about one-third of the Verses are published yet. A new volume, *Psalms and Songs*, is announced.

BIOGRAPHY AND CRITICISM

Douglas Day, *Malcolm Lowry, a Biography*, Oxford University Press, New York, 1973; London, 1974, with 50 illustrations. A very fully-documented work which provides a cumulation of previous biographical work, with a critical study of *Under the Volcano*.

Richard Hauser Costa, *Malcolm Lowry*, New York, 1972 (Twayne Authors' Series).

William H. New, *Malcolm Lowry*, Toronto/Montreal, 1971 (New Canadian Library).

Perle Epstein, *The Private Labyrinth of Malcolm Lowry: 'Under the Volcano' and the Cabbala*, New York, 1969.

Tony Kilgallin, *Lowry*, Erin, Ontario, Press Porcepic, 1973. Illustrated with cabbalistic symbols from the library of Stansfeld-Jones. Contains a very close study of the literary, cinematic and cabbalist background to *Under the Volcano*.

Much useful material was collected in the Lowry number of *Prairie Schooner*, xxxvii, 4 (Winter–Spring, 1964) and in *Malcolm Lowry, the Man and his Work*, ed. G. Woodcock (Canadian Literature Series) Vancouver 1971.

BIBLIOGRAPHY

J. Howard Woolmer, ed. *A Malcolm Lowry Catalogue*, New York, 1968.

The periodical *Canadian Literature* contains a full bibliography of poems, reprints and translations, and reviews by Earle Birney and Margerie Bonner Lowry (see no. 8, Spring 1961, 81–8; no. 9, Summer 1961, 80–4; no. 11, Winter 1962, 90–5; no. 19, Winter 1964, 83–9).

There are also select bibliographies in Day, New, Costa, Perle Epstein, and Kilgallin.

INDEX

Works, other than Malcolm Lowry's, are entered under the author. Names occurring in the text are not re-entered for the accompanying note.

167

Index